KU-592-319

Peter the Great

WILLIAM MARSHALL

947

LONGMAN
LONDON AND NEW YORK

Addison Wesley Longman Limited
Edinburgh Gate
Harlow, Essex CM20 2JE, England
and Associated Companies throughout the world.

Published in the United States of America
by Addison Wesley Longman Publishing Inc., New York

©Longman Group Limited 1996

All rights reserved; no part of this publication may be
reproduced, stored in a retrieval system, or transmitted
in any form or by any means, electronic, mechanical,
photocopying, recording, or otherwise without either the
prior written permission of the Publishers or a licence
permitting restricted copying in the United Kingdom issued
by the Copyright Licensing Agency Ltd.,
90 Tottenham Court Road, London W1P 9HE.

First published 1996
Second impression 1996

ISBN 0 582 00355 5 PPR

British Library Cataloguing-in-Publication Data

A catalogue record for this book is
available from the British Library

Library of Congress Cataloging-in-Publication Data

Marshall, William.
    Peter the Great/William Marshall.
        p. cm. -- (Seminar studies in history)
    Includes bibliographical references and index.
    ISBN 0-582-00355-5
    1. Peter I, Emperor of Russia, 1672–1725. 2. Russia--Kings and
rulers--Biography. 3. Russia--History--Peter I, 1689–1725.
I. Title. II. Series.
DK131.M27 1996
947'.05'092--dc20
    [B]   95-30682
                                                                      CIP

Set by 7 in 10/12 Sabon Roman
Produced through Longman Malaysia, PP

CONTENTS

EDITORIAL FOREWORD

Such is the pace of historical enquiry in the modern world that there is an ever-widening gap between the specialist article or monograph, incorporating the results of current research, and general surveys, which inevitably become out of date. *Seminar Studies in History* are designed to bridge this gap. The books are written by experts in their field who are not only familiar with the latest research but have often contributed to it. They are frequently revised, in order to take account of new information and interpretations. They provide a selection of documents to illustrate major themes and provoke discussion, and also a guide to further reading. Their aim is to clarify complex issues without over-simplifying them, and to stimulate readers into deepening their knowledge and understanding of major themes and topics.

NOTE ON REFERENCING SYSTEM

Readers should note that numbers in square brackets [5] refer them to the corresponding entry in the Bibliography at the end of the book (specific page references are given in italic). A number in square brackets preceded by *Doc.* [*Doc.* 5] refers readers to the corresponding item in the Documents section which follows the main text. Words which are defined in the Glossary are asterisked at first occurrence.

LIST OF MAPS

ACKNOWLEDGEMENTS

The publishers would like to thank the following for permission to reproduce copyright material: Franklin Watts, Inc. for two tables from *Russian Economic Development from Peter the Great to Stalin* by W. L. Blackwell and six extracts from *Peter the Great* edited by L. Jay Oliva © 1970 reprinted by permission of Prentice Hall/a Division of Simon & Schuster, Inc.

PREFACE

The demise of the Soviet Union in 1991, and continuing threats in 1995 to the unity of the Russian Federation itself, have increased the fascination and interest not only in the Soviet Union's origin at the 1917 Revolution but in its predecessor, the Russian Empire, which has now broken up into its constituent parts. Russia has shed not only Transcaucasia and Central Asia, but also its older possessions, the Ukraine (sometimes known as Little Russia*), White Russia* and the Baltic Republics, all acquired at or before Peter the Great's time. Of all the personalities who gave rise to the birth and development of the Russian Empire, none has intrigued historians more than Peter, not only because he ruled at the transition from ancient Muscovy* to modern Russia, but also because he was such a startling personality, so potent and yet so lacking in pomposity, abhorring grandeur of power, though recognising the sovereign's need to rule effectively. So awesome and yet so concerned with individuals, Peter was unique and has remained something of an enigma to posthumous generations. His drive for westernisation, with its attendant problems, cultural confrontation and lack of ease, is paralleled by the leaders of many Third World countries today, as they seek to modernise on western lines.

DATES, NAMES, POPULATION AND ARMY STATISTICS

1   **Dating** In the early eighteenth century there were two calendars current in Europe – the Julian, 'Old Style' (O.S.), still retained by England, Russia and Sweden, and the Gregorian, 'New Style' (N.S.), adopted by most European countries. Until 1700, Old Style was ten days behind New Style; after 1700 it was 11 days behind. There was an added complication in Sweden, which used a modified Old Style between 1700 and 1712, when it returned to Old Style. Thus Sweden in those years was ten days behind New Style, but one day ahead of Old Style [42 *p. 349*]. Documents from Swedish sources, such as the letters of James Jefferyes, often use Swedish style (S.S.).

2   **Placenames and personal names** Where a place or personal name has an accepted English form (Peter, Catherine, Charles, Courland), I have used it. Where, because of changes in territorial sovereignty, there has been a change of name, I have retained the name used in Peter's reign, but I have appended a topographical glossary for those who use contemporary maps or who like to visit historic sites. Transliteration from Cyrillic to Roman script can also cause additional confusion. I have followed the modern accepted form. Some earlier works will have slightly different western spelling.

3   **Population and army size** Historians differ widely. Statistical method in Peter's time was in its infancy. Contemporaries were frequently uncertain of figures themselves, even regarding army sizes. I have accepted the most recent estimates.

PART ONE: THE BACKGROUND

1 THE LAND AND ITS PEOPLE

R.T.C. LIBRARY, LETTERKENNY

At Peter's accession in 1682 Russia extended from the Arctic in the
north to the Caucasus in the south, from the borders of Poland in
the west to the wastes of Siberia in the east. Compared with the
later Russian and Soviet Empires, which also included Central Asia,
Transcaucasia and the Siberian hinterland as far as the Bering
Straits, it was small, but by contemporary Western standards it was
a vast incoherent mass of territory with rudimentary communications that made political control well nigh impossible. In the
sixteenth century, by conquering the Tatar Khanates of Kazan and
Astrakhan further south, Ivan IV had won control of the basin of
the Volga, Muscovy's vital southern artery. Steady movement
eastward continued from the 1580s onwards; in fact the first
intrepid explorers had reached the Pacific shores, where they
established one or two simple settlements in the 1630s.

The total population of Russia by Peter's accession is impossible
to estimate accurately. Recent historians have suggested a figure of
10 to 12 million [38 *p. 10*], about half the size of contemporary
France (21 million), but large compared with other Western states;
Spain (5.5 million), the British Isles (9 million), all Scandinavia (3
million) and the Low Countries (3.5 million) [29 *p. 82*].

A major drawback was Russia's landlocked position. Despite its
great size, it had no outlet to the Baltic. Ingria, Estonia and Finland
were still part of the Swedish Empire and Livonia belonged to
Poland. Russia's one outlet to the north – through the White Sea
port of Archangel, founded in 1584 – was icebound for over half
the year. In the south the Ottoman Empire and her vassal, the Tatar
Khanate of Crimea, blocked access to the Black Sea. In any case
there was immediately south of Muscovy a vast 300 or 400 mile
tract of empty uninhabitable steppe, peopled by marauding Tatars,*
descendants of the Mongols, who blocked any advance and
frequently attacked Russian settlements, capturing inhabitants to sell
as slaves in the markets of the Ottoman Empire.

In the west, Peter's father, Alexis (1645–76), had wrested two key places from the Poles – in 1654 Smolensk, 150 miles from Moscow, and in 1667 (by the Treaty of Andrussovo) Kiev, the principal city of the Ukraine and historic birthplace of Russian Orthodox culture. This success brought with it territory as extensive as England. By the earlier formal union agreed between its Cossack inhabitants and Moscow in 1654 Ukraine* with its more advanced culture became inextricably bound to Russia and was to remain so until 1991.

This whole vast area was by Western standards sparsely inhabited, underdeveloped and lacking in racial homogeneity. Compared with the West, 'fewer nations in the history of mankind were more poorly endowed by nature for economic growth and prosperity' [51 *p. xix*] than Russia. The soil round Moscow was extremely poor and crop rotation almost impossible, because of the harsh climate [51 *pp. xix–xx, 9*]. Furthermore, mineral resources, centres of trade and pockets of population were too widely spread. In the far north there were fur trappers and hunters. In the east, Siberian minerals lay untapped, and in the centre the harsh climate with its fierce winters and torrid summers hindered economic advance in all sorts of ways but especially in agriculture; the corn harvest for instance only gave a yield of a mere three or four times the seed sown. Transportation was a major problem. The mighty rivers Volga and Don flow contrariwise, away from St Petersburg and Moscow, which, as population grew, desperately needed the grain from the fertile south and, later, iron for industry. For many months each year, rivers and ports were blocked by ice and subsequently made impassable by spring floods. The rudimentary roads were likewise subject to the weather; it was not until the construction of the eighteenth-century canals and nineteenth-century railways that improved transport made the economy more workable. There were, it is true, the first signs of iron production in the north-west and at Tula, south of Moscow. There was also salt production on the shores of the White Sea at Perm and again in the south-east in the lower Volga. Tar, pitch, potash and wax were already regular exports. Grain was the main product of the Volga basin and of the lands south of Moscow towards the warm-water ports of the Black Sea. In the north-west linen and canvas were produced. The new trade route through the White Sea, opened up by Chancellor in the 1550s, caused a decline in the traditional route through Novgorod and Pskov. Foreign commerce was largely in the hands of foreigners who numbered a mere 3,000 in all Muscovy. Viewed with suspicion by xenophobic Russians, 1,700 were concentrated outside Moscow in the German or foreign suburb (*Nemetskaya Sloboda**) which was founded in 1652 and destined to be a centre of technological advance.

Population figures are always difficult to estimate, but it is certain that Russian towns were much smaller than those in the West. Even if a settlement with 1,000 inhabitants is regarded as a town, less than 5 per cent of the population was urban. Moscow, a large town with 150,000 to 200,000 inhabitants, was an exception and one of the largest in Europe. The seventeenth century was, however, a time of change for Russia. In the third quarter of the century the urban population increased by 24 per cent, but still remained small compared with the West. Fires and plagues were always a brutal hazard throughout Europe in this century, but especially so in Russia where wooden buildings predominated [*Doc. 1*]. In 1644–5, for instance, plague removed 80 per cent of the taxable population of Moscow.

Since locally elected town bodies had fallen into disuse a century earlier, towns were strictly controlled by the provincial governors (*voevody**). Even the most influential and richest merchants had little share in town government, despite the fact that they were restricted to their towns under the pretext of easing tax collection. Not until Peter established the *ratusha** of 1699 did 'merchants achieve freedom of movement. Even though they were adventurous overseas, Russian merchants showed surprisingly little enterprise within their own country, much to Peter's irritation, and, unlike their Western contemporaries, they contributed little to cultural life.

Russia's rudimentary political institutions, such as they were, also prevented rapid development. With semisacerdotal powers, tsars* were unrestricted autocrats, the source of all law, judges of life and death, and entitled to unlimited tax revenue and service. Centralisation increased still further, especially after the reign of Ivan III, the Great (1462–1505). Though the constant threat from Sweden and Poland made centralisation necessary, it hindered political development. Even the greatest *boyars,** originally the ancient landed class, were the tsar's abject subjects, his 'slaves'. As time passed, their aristocratic nature was diluted by the cluster of advisers from the minor landed gentry around the tsar, who were also given the title *boyar*. Even so, *boyars'* assent to legislation became purely nominal. When Peter abolished the *Boyarskaya Duma* (*boyars'* assembly), he was completing a process dating from Ivan III. Its colleague, the *Zemskii Sobor,** a representative meeting of townsfolk and all those who held land in return for service – the 'service men' (*sluzhilie lyudi*) – declined and ceased to exist after the

1650s. This meant that there was no effective constitutional check on the tsar's increasingly autocratic rule.

In turn, the concept of service for land was growing. Tsars increasingly used *boyars*, often uneducated and poor, as soldiers, sailors and diplomats, for whom service became a necessary means of livelihood. There was thus little distinction between the *pomestiya* estates, based on service, and *vochina*, those based on ancient hereditary right.

Serfdom was fundamental to Muscovy and a hindrance to change. As the *boyars* grovelled to the tsar, so the serfs grovelled to their masters, owing produce, labour-service or even money. Far from declining, serfdom was in fact extended and consolidated by Alexis in his *Ulozhenie*,* the new law-code of January 1649. Just when it was disappearing in the West, the rigid social control enforced by serfdom became the hallmark of Russian agrarian society, and the greatest hindrance to change.

2 MUSCOVY BEFORE PETER THE GREAT

How had Muscovy reached this stage? The Russians emerged from the mists of antiquity in the sixth and seventh centuries, but it was not until the Swedish Vikings, the *Rus,** settled in Novgorod in the early ninth century under the legendary Rurik, Prince of Novgorod, that much progress was made. Novgorod itself was soon to be overshadowed by Kiev, also colonised by Vikings (839). It was Vladimir (980–1015) who first created a coherent state out of the tribalism of the times, brought Orthodox Christianity to his territories and opened Russia to civilisation. Centuries of struggle were followed by the Mongol conquest, which brought the Kiev period to an end. After the capture of Kiev and neighbouring lands (1240) the khans* of the Golden Horde ruled Russia until 1480; Novgorod, though nominally independent, was their tributary. The Slav Princes of Moscow began to predominate in the fourteenth century, and in 1453 Moscow forced Novgorod into vassalage.

Ivan III, the first to style himself 'Great Prince and Autocrat of all Russia', finally threw off the Mongol yoke in 1480 and began to create a coherent Muscovite state. Between 1471 and 1488 he annexed Moscow's great rival, Novgorod, and in 1502 he captured Smolensk. His son, Vasily (1505–33), continued the work of consolidation. With the Ottoman conquest of Constantinople in 1453, Moscow became undisputed leader of Orthodox Christendom.

Vasily died in 1533, leaving the throne to his son, Ivan, later known as *Grozny* (i.e. stern or awesome), who was then only three years of age. In 1546, after a turbulent and traumatic childhood and adolescence, Ivan IV assumed full power with the new title of tsar (or Caesar). Administrative reforms early in the reign were followed by a reign of terror in which many *boyars* were executed and the remainder lost their power. Nevertheless, important Muscovite successes included the annexation of the Volga, the capture of Kazan (1547–52) and of Astrakhan (1556) and recognition of

Moscow by the Caspian Tatars. After 1557 Ivan turned north to try to capture the Baltic coastline. This aim became the cornerstone of his foreign policy, but it failed, through lack of a fleet to counter the opposition of other Baltic powers, Sweden, Denmark and Poland-Lithuania. After initial success in Latvia and Estonia, Ivan, by the time of his death, was left with only the eastern tip of the Gulf of Finland. Worn out and dissipated, he died on 18 March 1584. He had laid the foundations of Russian hegemony in Asia, but, despite the beginnings of regular trade with England (1555), his Baltic policy was a failure. The ever present threat of invasion from west and south remained.

The period after Ivan's death included the reign of Boris Godunov and the subsequent Time of Troubles from which the Romanov dynasty emerged in the person of Michael (1613–45), who in turn was succeeded by his son, Alexis, in 1645. Born in 1629, described traditionally by historians as a pious, remote, inaccessible figure, monastic in his habits, despite the autocratic, almost Byzantine, authority accorded to him, Alexis showed practical political and military sense. Internal instability made the early years uncertain; there were dangerous revolts in 1648–50 and 1662, and a Cossack revolt in 1667–71. Despite this, Alexis attempted to restructure the administration, imported foreign books, created new military formations under foreign guidance, built a fleet in the Caspian Sea with foreign shipwrights, and used Western technology for armaments and mining.

Alexis married Maria Miloslavskaya, from a minor noble family, early in the reign. Their two surviving sons, Feodor and Ivan, were both sickly; in fact, Ivan, who probably suffered from Down's syndrome, was mentally deficient and nearly blind. Sophia was the most notable of the six surviving daughters. After Maria's death in 1669, Alexis remarried. His new wife, Natalia Naryshkina, of an equally obscure noble family, had been brought up in the household of Artamon Matveev, formerly head of the *posolskii prikaz,** who was married to a Scot and, with his modern, Western ideas, was largely responsible for the reforms of the reign.

3   PETER'S EARLY LIFE AND CHARACTER

Natalia gave birth to Peter, her first child, on 30 May 1672. After Alexis's sudden death in 1676 rivalry between his two families rose to a peak. The new tsar, Feodor, recalled his uncle, Ivan Miloslavskii, leader of the faction, from virtual exile as *voevod* in Astrakhan and banished Matveev. Peter and his mother lived at Preobrazhenskoe,* three miles from the centre of Moscow, a favourite residence of Alexis and very close to the *Nemetskaya Sloboda*. In these formative years Peter was taught possibly by Paul Menzies of Aberdeen and later by Nikita Zotov. When tsar Feodor prematurely died in 1682, a new struggle between Naryshkins and Miloslavskys broke out, for it was clear that Ivan was incapable and yet Peter was still only aged nine. The Naryshkins seized power; the *Zemskii Sobor*, even though only a shadow of its former self, chose Peter as sole tsar; and Matveev was recalled. But the Naryshkins' success was short-lived. The Miloslavskys pressed the *streltsy** to revolt by persuading them that Feodor had been poisoned (see also page 65). On 25 May 1682 they attacked the Kremlin and hacked Matveev and other members of the Naryshkin clan to pieces in front of Peter's eyes. His dislike of the Kremlin remained with him all his life.

On 26 May a compromise was reached. The *Zemskii Sobor* agreed that Ivan and Peter should reign as senior and junior tsars respectively, with real power in the hands of Ivan's sister, Sophia. Her rule was certainly effective in many ways. Great Russia* and Ukraine were united in a customs union, while a treaty with Poland in 1686 confirmed Russia to be in full possession of Kiev. Furthermore, there was a concerted attempt to improve Russian influence in the West. Embassies were established in eleven capitals and, remarkably, the first ever European treaty with China was concluded in 1689. Prince Vasily Golitsyn, Sophia's lover and chief minister, whose reforms in so many ways prefigured those of Peter, was the author of the 'southern policy' to open a window on the

West through the Black Sea rather than risk confrontation with Sweden in the Baltic. There were plans to send young Russians abroad for education. Golitsyn also abolished the *mestnichestvo*,* the graded Muscovite table of aristocratic precedence, and made legal and judicial procedures more humane.

Peter and his mother, meanwhile, spent most of their time in Preobrazhenskoe, probably because of their traumatic earlier experience with the *streltsy*. There is no evidence that Sophia or Golitsyn forced them to remain there. Beginning with toy weapons and soldiers, by 1683 Peter had real firearms and developed a taste for warfare and military pursuits. So much so, that by the late 1680s he had recruited young men and boys to form his toy regiments (*poteshnie polki**) which later, as the *Preobrazhenskii** and *Semenovskii** regiments, were to feature so strikingly in his reign. Drilling and mock battles were the normal play and boyhood fun developed into adult military skill. Several of Peter's acquaintances during this period became prominent later in the reign. Many were foreigners, such as Franz Lefort from Geneva who had been in the foreign suburb since 1676, a swashbuckling womaniser who became Peter's special friend and whom he later made both admiral and general. Another was Patrick Gordon, an older, steady, reliable Scottish mercenary. The leading Russian was Alexander Menshikov, who is said to have started life as a pastrycook's boy; he was to feature as Peter's close companion after Lefort's death in 1699. The Dutchman, Franz Timmerman, taught Peter arithmetic, geometry, ballistics and fortification. His impact on Peter was seminal. He was with Peter when the young tsar first set eyes on an English boat; he later persuaded him to visit Archangel, where he could see the merchant ships arriving from Holland and England.

In summer 1689 Golitsyn returned from two expensive, but fruitless, campaigns to the Crimea. Peter's marriage to Evdokia Lopukhina, a girl of good family chosen by his mother in January 1689, provoked a denouement. He was of age and likely to have an heir. A rumour on 7 August that Sophia and Golitsyn planned to send the *streltsy* to Preobrazhenskoe to murder the Naryshkins, and even perhaps Peter himself, caused him to flee 40 miles to the Troitsa-Sergeev monastery. The Naryshkins, with Gordon's help, moved against Sophia's party. Golitsyn was arrested and exiled to the far north, where he died in 1714; Sophia was confined to the Novodevichii convent outside Moscow. Many of their adherents were hanged. Peter and Ivan now reigned jointly until the latter's death in 1696. Peter, aged seventeen in 1689, went back to his military activities in the German suburb; not until 1694 did he take full control of the government.

Peter was an unusual man and certainly an unusual tsar. Though when necessary he could play the traditional role [*Docs 2 and 10*], he was no remote pietistic figure, like some of his predecessors, emerging from the Kremlin merely for a pilgrimage. For Peter the Muscovite past represented ignorance, prejudice, inefficiency and corruption, whereas the West symbolised knowledge, progress and reason. He was above all a man of action, ruthless action, obsessive, impatient, almost manic. As one historian has written, 'Internally Peter the Great was constantly at the boiling point, possibly on the verge of breakdown or madness ... but in the world of political action and historical record, very few major actors played their roles with more confidence, consistency, and clarity of purpose' [*35 p. 5*]. His upbringing in Preobrazhenskoe had brought him into contact with the nearby foreign suburb, which captured his curiosity with its mingling of languages and cultures and the openness of its thought. Although he was never given a regular education, Peter later became proficient in Dutch and German and had some acquaintance with other tongues. A practical man rather than a thinker, he spent any spare time he had in carpentry, metalwork and shipbuilding; one of his passions was for woodturning and he took a lathe with him even on the Poltava campaign. Inspired by his visits to medical institutions and attendance at medical lectures in Amsterdam, he developed a lifelong fascination with medicine, particularly dentistry and surgery, which, to their horror, he practised on his courtiers. He usually carried a valise of surgical instruments with him, and if one of his operations was unsuccessful he was not averse to practising skilful pathological dissection of the cadaver. Intrigued too by his own dreams, he has left a detailed record of a number of them, unique for the period.

Equal to medicine was his love of the sea, which he first encountered with Timmerman at Archangel in 1694–5. In the words of the Russian historian, M.M. Bogoslovsky, there 'the roar of the waves, the sea air, the watery elements drew him in and with the years made themselves an urgent requirement for him. In him an elemental urge to the sea exploded' [*73 pp. 15–16*]. Later, in England (1698), he told his turner, Andrei Nartov, 'If I were not tsar, I would wish to be an admiral of Great Britain' [*73 p. 16*]. Whitworth, the British ambassador, reported in June 1712 that Peter, still a shipwright on the payroll, was spending a whole fortnight hard at work in the yard to speed the launching of a warship, the 'Poltava' [13 *pp. 230–1*].

Peter possessed unique self-confidence, even in the face of· the most disastrous defeats, by which he was never discouraged. He was always certain of the rightness of the course he had set. His determination and unbending will drove him on with his one aim – to enable Russia to catch up with the West. Impatient with the inertia which was the blight of Russian society, he was devoted to work – hectic hard work which was central to his life. It was by this standard that he judged others. Despite his own practical nature, he would often work on decrees and other documents from 5 a.m. to noon and from 4 p.m. to 11 p.m., like the enlightened despots later in the century. The hallmark of his working life was service to the state, for the common good (*obshchee blago*). First stressed in 1702, in a *ukaz** concerned with inviting foreign specialists into Russian service, this became increasingly emphasised as the years went by. Peter expected others to serve as he did, not only their superiors, but the common good. Even he, as tsar, served in the lower naval and military ranks while he gained experience; he did not allow himself promotion until he deserved it. Similarly, all those included in the Table of Ranks (see page 114) were expected to earn their position.

Volatile by nature, Peter's violent temper was terrifying, for he towered over others with his great height of six feet seven inches, and his face twitched in frightening convulsions when he was overwrought and frenzied. Sometimes this violence overflowed into physical assault – even his closest friends Menshikov and Lefort suffered and blood was drawn. Yet by the standards of the day Peter was not a cruel man; he used the death penalty sparingly, except in the cases of the revolt of the *streltsy* and his own son Alexis (see pages 65–6 and 73). His immediate heavy-drinking circle was boorish and he certainly lacked the refinements westerners expected of royalty. John Evelyn was appalled by his coarseness [*Doc. 6*]. Yet he was also a man of sensitivity, showing great affection for his second wife Catherine, an orphaned Lithuanian peasant [*Doc. 9*], and winning the regard of the Electress Sophia of Hanover [*Doc. 4*], despite her wish that 'his manners were a little less rustic'. In his later years especially, he loved gardening. In January 1699 an Austrian diplomat reported that Peter leapt from his dining table to assist in fighting one of the many Moscow fires [*9 p. 219*]; in 1724 he spent a whole night trying to rescue ordinary soldiers and sailors whose boat was in trouble.

Unlike many of his Western contemporaries, Peter preferred a simple lifestyle. Though autocratic and decisive as monarch, he was socially egalitarian in outlook. He enjoyed the company of people from all levels of society; indeed he was known to call unexpectedly at anyone's dwelling. His own dress was simple and usually shabby and sometimes stained with tobacco. Unlike future tsars, he never, for instance, donned the senior officer's uniform. Though eventually, after his visit to Paris in 1717, he saw the necessity of grandeur, he preferred modest dwellings, even to the extent of having false low ceilings in his own palace and rarely dining off gold and silver.

Nevertheless, he was aware of the importance of spectacle for public relations, which he showed in his frequent triumphal processions through Moscow after victories, the construction of a splendid new capital, and in 1722 the spectacular arrival at St Petersburg of the small boat in which he had first learnt to sail in 1688 and had christened 'the Mother of the Russian Navy'. To promote his prestige he had the Treaty of Nystad widely distributed in 6,000 copies. As with all monarchs in those days, he recognised the importance of portraiture for promoting a personality cult. As Henry VIII had had his Holbein and Charles I his Van Dyck, so Peter turned to Kneller (1697–8) and Carl Moor (1717), when he visited the West. Engravings of their portraits of him became widespread. The poet Pushkin (1799–1837) a century later in 1826 summarised Peter's versatility thus:

Now an academician, now a hero,
Now a seafarer, now a carpenter,
He, with an all-compassing soul,
Was on the throne an eternal worker.
[35 p. 5]

PART TWO: DESCRIPTIVE ANALYSIS

4   WAR

THE AZOV CAMPAIGN

Peter's reign was dominated by war with Sweden to the north and Turkey to the south. Of the two, Sweden seemed the more threatening, certainly between 1700 and 1709, but in reality Turkey was at all times the more difficult to defeat. At first Peter continued Golitsyn's 'southern policy', to make the Black Sea his 'window on the west'. His first significant operation was the attack on Azov, the Turkish fortress which guarded the outlet from the river Don (July–October 1695). War between Russia and Turkey had been simmering since 1689, but it was raids by the vassal Crimean Tatars on the Ukraine which gave Peter the necessary pretext for full-scale conflict. In addition he needed to make his presence felt during the negotiations between Austria and Poland (1694), in case he was either excluded from the talks or became a prey to their combined strength. Peter also played a crusading card. On the Azov expedition he used the very flag flown by Ivan IV when he had captured the Muslim fortress of Kazan (1552).

Typically, Peter himself served as a mere bombardier sergeant in the Preobrazhenskii regiment. Though his general, Boris Sheremetiev, had some small successes in the Dnieper Valley, divided command and poor technical skill brought about his eventual defeat. Peter's immediate response was characteristic. He raised a larger army under a single commander, Alexis Shein, and set about building an 'instant' war fleet – the first in Muscovite history and the harbinger of Peter's later obsession. As a model, he had a large 32-oared Dutch galley transported in sections overland from Archangel to Preobrazhenskoe. A further 27 small ships were moved overland from Moscow to Voronezh, his new shipbuilding site on the river Don. By means of this massive mobilisation 1,400 barges and two large 36-gun ships, the *Apostle Peter* and the *Apostle Paul*, were constructed. Fully involved himself in the work, Peter drew craftsmen from all over Russia, studied Venetian naval methods and manned his new fleet with 4,000 men, all of them perforce soldiers under the command of his general, Franz Lefort.

During this second campaign Peter himself again served in a humble role – as a galley captain. The fleet arrived at the Sea of Azov at the end of May 1696 and within two months had captured the fortress from the Turks. Peter immediately selected Taganrog nearby as the site for a naval base. This first success was the occasion for great rejoicing and the first of many formal triumphs through Moscow, with Peter walking the nine miles with the other galley captains behind Lefort's gilded carriage. The victory had the desired effect; Russia now had an outlet on to the Sea of Azov – an important first step to the Black Sea, still guarded by the Turkish fortress at Kerch. She was also a power to be reckoned with.

Despite his first victory, Peter realised that to survive at all he must achieve a rapid, efficient build up of armed forces as a shield against future Turkish or Swedish assaults and as a tool to open up outlets to foreign trade. He at once set himself a threefold task – to maximise manpower and resources for war; to acquire greater knowledge of Western technological expertise; and to mobilise a much broader Christian alliance against the Turks, whereby he could take Kerch and gain direct access to the Black Sea.

THE GREAT EMBASSY

So arose one of Peter's most spectacular adventures, the Great Embassy to the West, in many ways pivotal to the reign, despite its diplomatic failure. Its overt intention was to mobilise Western nations for a great crusade against the Muslim Turk, but Peter's unpublished object was to gather western technological expertise and to recruit foreign shipwrights, sailors and artisans for service in Russia. The embassy departed in March 1697 and returned in September 1698. In rather transparent disguise as Peter Mihailovitch, the tsar studied shipbuilding and worked in the dockyards of Amsterdam from September 1697; in his spare time he attended medical lectures at Leyden University and visited Ruysch's anatomical museum, hospitals and insane asylums [*Doc. 5*]. In January 1698 Peter moved to London, where he worked in the royal dockyards at Deptford and visited Woolwich Arsenal, Greenwich Hospital, the Tower, the Royal Society, the Mint, Portsmouth and Oxford university. While staying at Deptford, Peter and his boorish companions vandalised the house of the diarist, John Evelyn, in which they were staying and were described by Evelyn's servant as 'right nasty' [*Doc. 6*]. Nevertheless, Peter impressed William III by his zestful personality and Bishop Burnet of Salisbury [*Doc. 7*], William Penn, the Quaker, and Archbishop Tenison by his intellect and curiosity. Indeed, the multilingual rector of Lambeth, George Hooper, was inspired enough to buy a Russian dictionary, perhaps to act as interpreter. Peter left England on 3 May, but had to cut short his visit to Vienna in July, when news reached him that the *streltsy* were once again in revolt.

Diplomatically the embassy was a failure. Peter met cool disdain in Swedish-held Riga and was given only empty promises in Brandenburg-Prussia. Although his discussions with William III were cordial – William gave him his best yacht, the *Transport Royal* – they bore little practical fruit. Although they were fascinated by the tsar's odd mixture of zestful eccentricity, boorishness and intellectual curiosity, western rulers were preoccupied with the impending struggle over the Spanish succession. The most they would offer was mediation with the Ottoman Empire in the hope of some gain for themselves. In short, both time and circumstances were against the tsar, and, as far as diplomacy was concerned, he returned home empty-handed.

This was further substantiated by the treaty of Carlowitz (January 1699) between Austria, Poland and Venice on the one hand and the Turks on the other. Peter's hope of an anti-Turkish alliance was dashed, and therefore, after months of tough negotiation he agreed to a 30-year truce with the Turks (June 1700). This put an end, for the time being, to his hopes of taking Kerch and achieving access to the Black Sea. However, he kept Azov and the new dockyard at Taganrog, free of dues to the Crimean Tatars. He also gained the right to diplomatic representation at the Porte,* the Turkish court. Nevertheless Peter felt ill-used. The time, energy and resources devoted to the new Azov fleet seemed to have been wasted. He blamed Austria for this, and relations between the two states remained cool throughout his reign.

THE STRUGGLE AGAINST SWEDEN

Frustrated in his Turkish ambitions, Peter now turned his attention northwards, to the threat from Sweden. Despite the long efforts of Ivan IV and Alexis to break out to the Baltic, Sweden's control of Karelia, Ingria and now Livonia was as tight as ever. However, the omens seemed more propitious for Peter than they had done for the Turks, for anti-Swedish feeling was rife throughout northern

Europe, particularly in Denmark, Brandenburg-Prussia and Poland-Lithuania all of whom had suffered at the hands of Gustavus Adolphus (1611–32) and Charles X (1654–60). Inside Sweden too there was unrest; Swedish nobles resented the absolutist tendencies of Charles XI (1660–97) and the enforced surrender of their lands. Sweden's enemies also took comfort from the fact that Charles XI's successor, Charles XII, was a fourteen-year-old boy, whose hold on power appeared uncertain and whose military ability was negligible. Success for an anti-Swedish coalition therefore seemed likely, though events were to prove otherwise.

The Danes under Frederick IV (1699–1730) and the Saxons under Augustus, their ambitious, shrewd, but double-dealing Elector (now also King of Poland 1697–1704 and 1707–33) had already been allied against Sweden since March 1698. Frederick wanted Holstein-Gottorp, and Augustus dreamed of the recovery of Livonia. They had invaded these territories respectively in February and March 1699. Peter secretly allied with Augustus. If successful, Augustus was to have Livonia and Peter, Ingria. As a cloak for his designs, while awaiting confirmation of peace with Turkey to guard his rear, Peter simultaneously reaffirmed the Russo-Swedish Treaty of Kardis of 1661. However, as soon as news of the successful conclusion of the 30-year truce with Turkey reached Peter, he declared war on Sweden in August 1700.

His timing could not have been more unfortunate, for on the very day that war was declared the Danes collapsed under Charles's lightning attack across the Sound. With support from English and Dutch fleets, the eighteen-year-old king with 11,000 troops forced the Danes to surrender outside Copenhagen. Under the terms of the Treaty of Travendal, Frederick IV withdrew from the war. Peter and Augustus were left alone to pursue the struggle against Sweden.

Elated by his success, Charles turned east, where two Swedish fortresses were in peril. Augustus was threatening Riga in Livonia, while Peter was threatening to take Narva and thus divide Livonia from Ingria. Dressed as an officer in the *Preobrazhenskii* regiment, Peter laid siege with 40,000 men. But in October 1700, Charles, ignoring autumn storms, landed his army of 11,000 men in Livonia, where the nobility were largely loyal to him. Despite weariness, cold and hunger, the Swedes were in high spirits after their successful campaign against Augustus. On 20 November they appeared before Narva, with Rehnskjöld in command, and routed the Russians in a heavy snowstorm; Charles's victory was total. Ragnhild Hatton has shown that recent scholarship puts the Russian loss at between 8 and 10,000 casualties, as against a Swedish total of 2,000 [42]. So many prisoners were taken by the Swedes that all non-Russian soldiers and Russian privates had to be released. In the panic Peter lost all his artillery, including 145 cannon and 32 mortars. His cavalry fled without fighting; his foreign officers and even the new infantry proved hopeless.

For Peter, Narva was a total disaster, especially as the road to Moscow now lay open to Charles. The Swedes initially planned to take it, but wiser counsels prevailed. A winter campaign into Russia was risky with many of the troops sick and no hope of reinforcements until the spring. Moreover, France, now further entangled in the Spanish succession, dropped her support for Sweden. Charles therefore turned towards Poland and for the next six years was embroiled in the quagmire of Polish politics. This was Peter's salvation.

Peter recognised his luck. He was now free to regroup, reform and reequip his army and prepare for another attempt to detach Ingria from Swedish control. To do this he had to keep Augustus, unreliable and devious as he was, in the field against Sweden. Peter met him at Birsen in February 1701, offered him 14 to 20,000 troops, gunpowder, a subsidy and an assurance that Russia only claimed Ingria, not Swedish-held Livonia and Estonia.

Charles's Polish involvement forced him to relax his grip on the Baltic provinces. This was Peter's chance and he took it. In October 1702 he gained control of Lake Ladoga and captured the Swedish fortress of Nöteborg (22 October), aptly renaming it Schlüsselburg or 'key-fortress'; it opened the door to future expansion. The Russians moved swiftly. Peter himself with Menshikov advanced down the Neva and took Nyenskans, while Sheremetiev swept through Estonia and Livonia. By the end of summer 1703 Peter controlled much of the Baltic coastline. In the following year, Dorpat in Livonia fell, followed by Narva in August. Though Sheremetiev's thrust into Poland with 50 to 60,000 men was halted at Gemauerhof in July 1705, most of Courland was in Russian hands by 1706. But this was not the end. Russia and Sweden were locked in a struggle with no possibility of compromise. Peter was determined to maintain his Baltic outlet at all costs; Charles was equally determined to seal Peter off again.

The tables suddenly turned. In 1706 Charles XII unexpectedly invaded Saxony, Augustus's hereditary domains, forcing him to accept the Peace of Altanstradt in September. Augustus now had to surrender the Polish throne to Charles's protégé, Stanislas Lecsynski, and abandon the Russian alliance. At a stroke Charles had isolated Russia, whose situation was once again critical. Moreover, he could again count on support in the West, where belligerents began bidding for his backing in the War of Spanish Succession, now at its height.

Meanwhile, Peter faced widespread disaffection at home, created by military conscription, forced labour and heavy taxation. There was a Bashkir revolt in the Urals in 1705, a mutiny in Astrakhan in 1706, and a lengthy, dangerous rebellion of the Don Cossacks* in 1707. Furthermore, he was without Feodor Golovin, his able foreign minister, who had died in August 1706, just when his diplomatic skills were most needed. The future looked black, particularly as no help was likely from the West. To save Russia, Peter would have to defeat Charles on his own. But his immediate problem was to prepare defences against an impending Swedish invasion. In 1707–8 he withdrew his troops from the newly acquired Baltic provinces, leaving devastation behind him. Germans from Dorpat, suspected of being pro-Swedish, were deported by sledge to Vologda in inner Russia. Moscow itself was fortified.

CHARLES XII'S INVASION OF RUSSIA

Late in 1707 Charles was ready. Historians still debate the size of his main fighting force. The traditional figure of 44,000 men has been challenged by recent research of Ragnhild Hatton and Stewart Oakley which mostly supports a figure of 33,000 fighting men, perhaps with 11,000 noncombatants in support [42 and 30]. Charles also had about 11,400 in the Baltic provinces at Riga under Lewenhaupt and a further 14,000 in Finland standing by to attack St Petersburg. The reformed Russian army has been estimated at 135,000. With the victory of Narva still fresh in their minds, the Swedes were over-confident; to them the Russians were 'a rabble'. Nevertheless, Charles made overtures to Turkey, whose client, the Crimea, which bordered the Ukraine, was already in revolt against Peter. Crossing the frozen Vistula in January 1708, Charles reached the river Dnieper the following July and with 20,000 men defeated the 38,000 Russians at Holowczyń (Golovchin) on 3 July (S.S.). But the Russians were no longer the rabble Charles had known at Narva; indeed, an English observer, Jefferyes, serving with Charles, regarded them as better disciplined and more courageous than the Saxons [*Doc. 11*]. Peter's scorched earth strategy hit the Swedes hard; the scarcity of food in the winter cold and summer heat, the poor roads and a hostile Russian population reduced their advance to a mere eight to ten kilometres a day. Charles quickly realised his urgent need for Lewenhaupt's 12,500 troops already on the move from Riga, but they were slowed down by the same factors that impeded Charles.

Charles therefore changed tack. Abandoning his drive on Moscow in mid-September, he moved south into the Ukraine where food was more readily available and Ukrainian and Turkish support likely. However, Lewenhaupt's relieving force was heavily defeated in late September (O.S.) 1708 by Peter and Menshikov at Lesnaya (Lesna in Polish), the tsar himself commanding the Preobrazhenskii and Semenovskii regiments. Lewenhaupt escaped to rejoin Charles, but with only a demoralised, bedraggled remnant of 6,000 men, no artillery and no supplies. This was a remarkable turn of the tide, the first sign of things to come. Little wonder Peter later called Lesnaya 'the Mother of Poltava' [48 *p. 70*].

Soon afterwards Mazepa, the Cossack *hetman*,* badly miscalculated by declaring for the Swedes, but less than half his 5,000 men followed him. In November 1708 Menshikov took his capital, Baturin, by storm, ruthlessly massacred its inhabitants and razed it to the ground. Ukraine subsequently submitted, as her dreams of independence slipped away. Charles and his men now faced the Ukrainian winter – which turned out to be the harshest in living memory – amid a population whose antipathy was steadily growing. Peter spent the winter at Voronezh reequipping his fleet. By the spring his newly reinforced Azov garrison and a powerful display of naval power had persuaded the sultan to order the Crimean Tatars to remain neutral. This meant that Charles was without allies.

POLTAVA

In May 1709 Charles lost another ally, the Zaporozhian* Cossacks, whose headquarters on the Sech was totally destroyed by Menshikov. Weakened by the winter, without adequate artillery and supplies since Lesnaya, but still labouring under the delusion of Swedish invincibility, Charles was as impetuous as ever. In late April 1709 he decided to besiege Poltava [*Doc. 12*]. The Russian army, better seasoned than at Narva, with Peter himself for once taking supreme command, arrived in June. Peter even considered coming to terms with Charles, despite Russian morale being high and Swedish low. But although Charles was weakened by a serious foot wound and high fever, he launched an attack at dawn on 8 July 1703

R.T.C. LIBRARY, LETTERKENNY
947.105

against an army twice the size and with superior artillery. The four-hour battle proved to be the turning point of the war. Charles's stretcher was hit by bullets; after he transferred to a horse, this too was shot from under him. Likewise Peter was active; indeed a small bullet passed through his hat, another through his saddle and another glanced off his neck. In the event, the 40,000 Russians with their 75 guns decisively defeated the 22,000 Swedes [*Docs. 13* and *14*].

Two days later the defeat was turned into a rout at Perevolochna on the left bank of the Dnieper, where Lewenhaupt, weak with illness, surrendered the remaining Swedish troops (over 13,000) to Menshikov. The previous night Charles, still sick, had been persuaded to escape across the Dnieper to Bender in Turkish territory, to negotiate for Tatar help. He was appalled by the news of Lewenhaupt's surrender, whom he thought 'must have taken leave of his senses' [*42 p. 305*].

Peter later described Poltava as 'a very outstanding and unexpected victory – in a word the whole army has met with Phaeton's destiny' [*Doc. 13*]. 'Now the final stone has been laid of the foundation of St Petersburg' [*48 p. 73*]. In December 1709 the principal Swedish captives were made to march through Moscow in Peter's triumph. The review was taken by Prince Romodanovskii as mock-tsar; Peter as a colonel followed the two marshals, Sheremetiev and Menshikov. Firework displays, eulogies and medals all marked the occasion. It was indeed the turning point [*Docs. 13* and *14*], but the rejoicing proved premature. Twelve years of hard struggle lay ahead.

RUSSIA'S EMERGENCE AS A MAJOR POWER

The decisiveness of Poltava transformed Peter's reputation at home and in Europe. The colossal expense of his army reforms and expansion were justified to a disaffected public. In central Europe, Poland became little more than a satellite. Peter expelled Stanislas Leczynski and restored Augustus in October 1709. Seven years later Peter intervened in the struggle between Augustus and his nobles and weakened Poland still further by negotiating a limitation of her army to 24,000 men. In 1710, by another diplomatic coup, Peter made an ally of Elector Georg Ludwig of Hanover, soon to be George I of Britain, by agreeing to support his claim to Bremen and Verden. He also prompted the Danes to reenter the war and invade Scania in June 1710.

A0019112

The transformation in the Baltic was seismic. In June 1710 Apraksin, with Peter as rear admiral 'Mihailov', captured the fortress of Viborg (Viipuri), thereby securing St Petersburg. This gave Russia control of Karelia and led to the reoccupation of Ingria. Sheremetiev then took both Reval and Riga, which meant that Livonia was back in Russian hands. Meanwhile the neutrality of Courland was obtained through the marriage of Peter's niece, Anna, to its duke. Further west the impact of Poltava was as marked. Russia was no longer peripheral, and Peter found himself included in central councils of Europe – a marked contrast with the situation at Carlowitz in 1699. The western powers, to whom Charles XII had seemed invincible, were stunned [*Doc. 13*]. Whitworth, the British ambassador, even recommended Peter to his government in August 1709 as a possible mediator in the War of Spanish Succession. Sunderland, the Secretary of State, in reply, suggested that Russia should join the Grand Alliance [38 *p. 62* and *184n*]. Austria and Prussia also made overtures to the triumphant tsar. But Peter, cautious as ever, took great care not to risk his new position. Poland was too unstable, Sweden had not yet made peace, and there were also troubles at home.

Turkey also remained a danger. Between 1700 and 1709 Peter had worked hard to keep her at peace, but his victory over Charles alarmed the Turks. Furthermore, Charles, thwarted in his planned return to Sweden by Russian and Polish control of the land routes, plague in Hungary and the dangers of the sea passage, collaborated to stir up trouble with the exiled Ukrainian hetman, Mazepa, and the Crimean khan,* Devlet Girei. In spite of desperate overtures to the Porte by Tolstoi, the Russian envoy, the sultan declared war in November 1710.

Peter delayed his own declaration of war until March 1711. Hoping to raise the Balkans in revolt, he invaded the sultan's Christian provinces of Moldavia and Wallachia, urging Slav Christians, the Serbians and Montenegrins, to throw off the Muslim yoke. It was a risky gamble. The Balkans did not respond as he had hoped and supplies were short. In mid-July, at Stanelishte on the River Pruth, Peter found himself and his army of 45,000 surrounded by 100,000 Turks and their allies. The situation was disastrous, annihilation likely, his own capture possible. As he later put it, the Turks 'had the bird in their hand there' [45 *p. 562*]. So desperate was Peter that he was prepared to sacrifice much – even, if necessary, his Baltic conquests. 'Agree to anything, except slavery', he told his emissary. The Turks, however, had their own problems, they needed a quick peace, and settled for much less. Even so, Peter had to give up all he had gained from the Turks since 1698, including Azov, Taganrog and the southern fleet. He also had to promise not to interfere in Poland and to allow Charles XII free passage back to Sweden [*Doc. 15*]. Yet by the Peace of Pruth Peter himself was left at liberty with his Baltic conquests intact [*Doc. 15*].

The Peace of Pruth turned out to be a blessing in disguise. Peter no longer had to fight on two fronts, especially after confirmation of the Peace by the Treaty of Adrianople in June 1713, though he had to recognise Cossack and Zaporozhian independence. The timing of his withdrawal from Azov and Poland was a useful bargaining counter to secure the expulsion of Charles. The Swedish king eventually left Turkish territory in September 1714, with a party of 130, and reached Stralsund, in disguise, the following November. Peter spent the ensuing two years mostly in Germany, cementing alliances and making arrangements for the marriage of the Tsarvich Alexis to Princess Charlotte of Brunswick-Wolfenbüttel. As well as taking the waters at Carlsbad, Pyrmont and Spa, Peter had a meeting with the philosopher, Leibniz, whose later correspondence had considerable influence on him. He was in Russia for only a short spell early in 1712, when he married his second wife, Catherine [*Doc. 8*].

Using his Baltic fleet, made up mostly of 99 galleys* manned by Greeks and Italians, Peter turned his attention to Finland in 1714. With their shallow draught they were ideal for manoeuvring in the shallow waters and landing an invasion force, and by May 1714 Russian troops had overrun the Finnish coast as far as Åbo, capturing Helsinki on the way. The campaign culminated in the great naval victory of Hangö Udd on 6 August 1714, won entirely by galleys against ships-of-the-line* – a personal victory for Peter and his commanding Admiral, Apraksin. The fleet went on to capture the Åland Islands, thereby posing a threat to Stockholm itself, and in September Russian galleys raided and burnt Umeå on the Swedish mainland.

Peter's attempt to build up a system of alliances was thwarted by fears of Russia replacing Sweden as the dominant power in the Baltic. These fears – which led to his exclusion from participation in the capture of Stralsund in 1715 and Wismar in 1716 – were intensified by the marriage of Peter's niece, Catherine, to the Duke of Mecklenburg in 1716 and his rumoured plan for constructing a Kiel canal through to the North Sea to avoid the Sound dues.

In July 1716 Peter was in Copenhagen, preparing to invade Sweden with 50,000 troops and Anglo-Danish support. By mid-September, however, he had changed his mind. The campaigning season was too far advanced, Charles had returned and, more important, Peter felt he could not risk putting Russian troops on Swedish soil, where they would be totally dependent for logistical support on the British and Danes whose loyalty he doubted. As a sop to the Danes he withdrew his troops to Mecklenburg, but this only intensified German antagonism, so he withdrew from there too in the summer of 1717.

With his former allies hostile to him, Peter decided on a radical change of plan. He would try to win over France, Sweden's traditional ally. He began with a six-week tour of Paris in May 1717, in which visits to the Sorbonne, the Academy of Sciences and the Gobelin tapestry manufactory, served as a cover for his diplomatic overtures. These, however, yielded little. The most the French would do was to stop subsidising Sweden and to persuade Charles XII to undertake negotiations for a settlement. The Russo-French agreement, such as it was, was embodied in the Treaty of Amsterdam in August 1717.

By January 1718 Peter was back in Moscow. Long years of war and internal pressures in Sweden forced her to negotiate. In May 1718 Swedish and Russian representatives met at Lövö on the Åland Islands. Russia was represented by a Russianised Scot, James Bruce, one of Peter's leading military advisers, and Heinrich Ostermann, his foremost diplomat, renowned for his incorruptibility. Sweden's team was led by Görtz of Holstein-Gottorp, Charles's leading foreign policy adviser. The talks lasted for eighteen months, but from as early as August 1718 there was provisional agreement for Peter to keep all the Baltic provinces in return for Finland and most of Karelia, which were to revert to Swedish control. However, both sides had second thoughts, and Peter, fearing the loss of Western support, decided to withdraw.

Charles's sudden and unexpected death on 11 December 1718 (N.S.), while besieging the Norwegian fortress of Frederiksten, made matters worse for Peter, for the reins of power in Sweden were seized by the militant, anti-Russian party. Charles's successor – his sister, Ulrika Eleanora, with her husband, Frederick of Hesse-Cassel – favoured alliance with Britain and continued war with Russia. Görtz and his conciliatory group were removed and Görtz himself executed. The Åland talks became an irrelevance, but Peter still had all the cards in his hands in the shape of the territory he had gained and his acknowledged military and naval strength.

British attempts to prevent Russian dominance of the Baltic by sending a naval force under Sir John Norris in three successive years (1719–21) failed, for his mighty ships-of-the-line could not cope with the fast-moving shallow-draught Russian galleys. In 1719 they could not even prevent the Russian galleys from landing 6,000 troops in the Stockholm archipelago and causing havoc within a few miles of Stockholm itself [*Doc. 16*]. This, coupled with financial weakness after the South Sea Bubble and fear of Jacobite activity, led George I in November to press the Swedes to reopen negotiations. Representatives of both sides met again in February 1721, this time at Nystad/Uusikaupunki in Finland. Peter was in a strong position, for possession was nine points of the law. He had 25,000 men already in Finland with another 11,000 about to arrive. With his 48 ships-of-the-line, 300 galleys and troops, he kept up pressure by continuing raids into north Sweden during the Nystad conference, which officially opened on 22 May. Five thousand men were landed and ravaged the whole north Swedish coastline, and Umeå was burnt once again in the summer of 1721. Sweden had little choice but to accept Peter's terms, and in September 1721 the Treaty of Nystad brought hostilities to an end [*Doc. 17*].

Under the terms of the treaty Peter retained Estonia, Livonia, Ingria and part of Finland, including the fortress of Viborg and the province of Karelia (he already controlled Courland through his niece's marriage). In return, he merely had to grant Sweden a payment of 1.5 million roubles and a qualified right to purchase 50,000 roubles worth of Livonian grain, duty free. He also agreed not to intervene in Swedish internal affairs. Russian domination of the Baltic was now confirmed, even though it was not until 1808 that the rest of Finland passed into Russian hands [*Doc. 17*].

Now that the Great Northern War was over, Peter was free to pursue his aims further afield. Some historians have seen Peter's policies of marriage alliances, even with the French Bourbons, as aiming at European hegemony. It was certainly the case that for the first time Russia had embassies at most courts in Europe. Moreover, the title of Emperor (*Imperator*), which Peter assumed in 1721, gave Russia new status as an integral part of the European system.

But Peter had more far-reaching aims. He hoped to follow up the Treaty of Nerchinsk (1689), negotiated by Feodor Golovin, the first 'equal treaty' ever made by a European power with China. This had defined the Amur river as the border between China and Muscovy and opened up trade. Peter sent embassies to Peking in 1692 and

1719, for he was wise enough not to risk an open challenge to Chinese power at a time when the Qing dynasty, under the Emperor Kangxi (1661–1722), was at its height. His tactics were successful, for a new treaty of 1728 gave Russia the right to send one trade caravan to Peking every three years and to maintain a Russian church in the Chinese capital for the use of the small number of Russian inhabitants.

Expeditions to the Irtysh river in search of gold, and to the khan of Khiva and the emir of Bukhara (1716–17), were both unsuccessful, the latter ending in annihilation. Nevertheless, other eastern probes met with some success. Expeditions in the direction of Persia were useful, not only by opening up trade and a route to India, but also by directing Turkish attention from the Great Northern War. Subsequent threats to Russian merchants from the instability of Persia and Transcaucasia spurred Peter to invade the Caspian area with an army of 30,000 soldiers and 5,000 sailors in 1722. He captured Derbent and the Persian port of Resht, and although he failed to reach the Georgian capital, Tblisi, he did capture Baku in 1723. However, Russia found the Caspian seaboard too costly to maintain and it was abandoned in the 1730s.

In Siberia, Peter extended the frontiers into the area north of China by taking the Kamchatka peninsula and the Kurile Islands. It was at his request that the Danish navigator, Bering, set out on the first of his Arctic expeditions, which led to the discovery of the straits between Russia and Alaska. Contact with India was also a major aim. This was first pursued by sending merchants overland to the Mogul Emperor, Aurungzeb, but in 1723 Peter planned an expedition to Madagascar as a stepping-stone to India. This proved to be abortive, however, for the ships were so faulty that they never left the Baltic.

5 PETER'S ARMY AND NAVY

THE ARMY

Peter was at war for a total of over 28 years between 1695 and 1723. It is hardly surprising that military matters should have dominated his reign and his thinking. His unusual interest at an early age in the art of war made life in the German suburb an apt preparation. A powerful army and navy were essential for defence, particularly after 1703, when the strategically exposed St Petersburg needed protecting. Except for a brief spell, never before had the army reached 100,000, nor had there been a navy of any significance. The sheer magnitude of Peter's military and naval expansion had massive repercussions on Russia's economy and her industrial and social infrastructure. Indeed, warfare absorbed most of the revenue – 75 per cent by 1701 and as much as 80 per cent in 1710, only reducing to 67 per cent by 1725. The burden was borne entirely by the Russian people, with no foreign loans. To withstand the immediate threat from Sweden and Turkey, rapid escalation of military might was essential. Such urgency suited Peter's stormy, impetuous personality. Nevertheless, there was nothing entirely new in the nature of Peter's reforms. Ivan III, Ivan IV and Alexis had all sought to assimilate foreign technology and military expertise. Even recruitment of foreign troops was no novelty.

Peter's achievement was to build an integrated force out of the many disparate elements he found at his accession. The oldest section, the feudal cavalry, manned by landowners and their retainers, was of limited value because it only owed restricted service each year. Even by 1600 it was obsolete and a century later came in for severe criticism in Pososhkov's essay *On the Conduct of the Army* [67 p. 119]. More significant were the *streltsy*, part palace-guard, part standing-army, comprising 22 regiments of 1,000 each. However, by 1690 this force, over 140 years old, had also decayed into a hereditary, privileged, archaic group who were a brake on any reform. More recent still were the newer Western-style units. Known as 'troops of foreign formation*', they were first formed in the 1630s by patriarch* Filaret, Michael Romanov's father. Equipped with muskets and still led by Western, mostly German, officers, they numbered perhaps 89,000 out of a total army strength of 130,000 by the 1680s. Though they were undoubtedly far more effective than the older units, Peter regarded them as insufficient against the ever-present threat of Sweden and the potentially greater danger posed by Turkey. In any case, despite their successes against the Turks in the 1680s and 1690s, they were in fact being run down on grounds of expense.

In 1698 Peter embarked on his reforms with the issue of new regulations, written in part by himself, but it was not until late 1699 that his major army reorganisation went into top gear. By a *ukaz** of 8 November 1699 volunteers were offered eleven roubles a year in addition to a food allowance, a handsome sum at the time. These volunteer forces were in effect a development of Peter's boyhood 'toy regiments', *poteshnie polki*, of the 1680s, the *Preobrazhenskii, Semenovskii, Lefortovskii** and the *Gordonovskii** regiments. In the 1690s, after training under foreign officers, often in competitive military exercises against the *streltsy*, and experience in the Azov campaign of 1696, they became the first four regiments of the Imperial Guard.

Another *ukaz*, issued on 17 November 1699, laid the basis for conscription. Landowners were ordered to provide one footsoldier for each group of 50 peasant households and one cavalryman for each 100. Gentry (*dvoranye*) in the civil service, widows and retired men had to recruit at the rate of one for every 30 peasant households; clergy and substantial landowners one for every 25. In order to safeguard crop production, these recruits were not to be taken from among the agricultural serfs or from the original non-Slavic, so-called 'black peasant'*, communities, but from the household serf population. A significant, but unwelcome, innovation – for it was not stipulated in the *ukaz* – was that conscripts were to serve for life. Hence Peter's nickname for them – his 'immortals'. This system lasted in roughly this form until 1874.

Enlistment initially fell far short of Peter's target of 60 to 80,000, for he only gathered just over 32,000 men, of whom between one-quarter and one-third were volunteers. Nevertheless, he was able to create 32 new infantry regiments in 1698–9 and another 39 in 1700. Until 1700 most officers were foreign, but after that Peter began commissioning Russians.

The massive loss of 7 to 12,000 men at Narva forced Peter to raise a further 47 infantry and 5 grenadier regiments. He also recalled 25,000 of the old-style cavalry to Moscow and gave some former *streltsy* a role in field and garrison duties.

Regular recruitment under new regulations did not get under way until February 1705. Following the Swedish pattern, physically fit married men between the ages of fifteen and twenty were enlisted, at the rate – higher than in 1699 – of one from each set of twenty peasant households, and were called for the first time by the Western word *rekrut** (instead of the customary *datochnnye lyudi*). Though 44,500 recruits were raised in 1705, the numbers declined as the years passed. Recent work by J. L. Keep reveals that about 138,000 men were enrolled between 1701 and 1709, far fewer than the inflated estimates of the nineteenth-century historians (230,000) and Klyuchevsky's 300,000 [67].

After Poltava, levies declined still further, but even so the military establishment in 1711 allowed for 42 field infantry regiments (62,000 men), garrison troops of two dragoon and 30 infantry regiments (58,000), and 33 cavalry regiments (44,000), as well as an artillery regiment. The growth of artillery was notable, and by 1713 eighteen Russian fortresses had a total of 4,000 cannon. The Turkish war (1711) caused a new flurry of activity. In addition to the regular levy, Moscow proprietors had to hand over one out of every three of their household servants; this yielded another 50,000 or so recruits. Ten further levies between 1713 and 1725 produced 153,000 in total, which included priests surplus to church needs. The total number of men recruited in Peter's reign must have been in excess of 300,000. Richard Hellie estimates that at its greatest the military and naval establishment was about 265,000, one of the largest in Europe [66 *p. 95*]. Recruitment on this scale was not without its critics: in 1701, for instance, Pososhkov, the writer and future entrepreneur, in his essay *On the Conduct of the Army*, put forward the alternative of a small highly trained cadre. However, Peter stuck to his course and built up not simply a large, but a regularly trained and permanent force. The break with the past was accentuated by the introduction of new German-style uniforms.

The significance of this massive enlargement of the army for governmental administration is debatable. Some historians, such as Michael Roberts [62 *p. 67*, 70 *p. 22*], claim that it led to streamlining and development. Others, such as Jeremy Black, doubt this. Military change, for Black, was a consequence, not a cause of development [62 *p. 67*]. In fact, David Parrott goes so far as to say that, in the West, army size, far from being a catalyst for state centralisation, led to increased delegation to entrepreneurs, at least in the early stages [70 *p. 27*]. Historians are not in agreement on this subject and more work needs to be done. All that can be asserted with certainty is that in 1701 Peter established the Department of Military Affairs (*Prikaz Voennykh Del'*), which was replaced successively by the War Chancery (*voennaya kantselyariya*) in 1706 and the War College (*krigs kollegiya*) in 1719. In 1716 Peter also issued the Military Regulations (*Ustav voinskii**), an administrative code for the whole army, which typically he helped to formulate.

OFFICER RECRUITMENT AND WEAPONRY

The massive increase in size of Peter's army led to two important consequences: an increased demand for officers of high calibre and an improvement in weaponry. The paucity of competent officers was a major problem. In July 1700, in eight new regiments Peter only had 78 well-trained officers out of an establishment of 264 captains and subalterns, and 33 of these were foreigners. In fact, Adam Weide, responsible for reorganisation and himself a German, tried to make up for this shortfall by recruiting more foreigners, despite their unpopularity with the troops and, often, their poor previous records. Peter also selected sons of nobles to go to the West for training under famous generals, such as Eugène of Savoy. However, most Russian officers received their training in the guards units, the *Preobrazhenskii* and *Semenovksii* regiments. Practical competence was paramount and edicts of 1711, 1719 and 1724 insisted on all potential officers serving time in the ranks. In Peter's last years these officer-training units were turning out between 200 and 400 officers a year.

In addition, Peter provided specialist training for potential and serving officers. He founded the first artillery school in 1701, and others followed. A school for army surgeons was founded in 1707, for engineers in 1712 at Moscow and in 1719 at St Petersburg. Though the officer cadres remained weak by western standards down to the 1917 Revolution, Peter's achievement in officer training was substantial. As a result of this and the reduced Swedish threat he was able, by 1721, to exclude foreigners even from the technical arms. The continuance of the Petrine system after his death was assured. Indeed, the concept of service became part and parcel of Russian life.

To match the expansion and improved training of personnel there were also rapid advances in tactical techniques and in weaponry. The disaster at Narva had shown that the hasty reforms of the late 1690s were insufficient, so with Weide's help Peter made a fresh start. First, he introduced new training manuals. The existing one, written before 1647 and modelled on Jacob von Wallhausen's *Kriegkunst Zu Fuss* of 1615, had been rendered obsolete by the Thirty Years War. The old tactics of musketeers, pikemen and line formation had been revolutionised by technical improvements in artillery and infantry weapons, especially the flintlock* and the bayonet*. Peter's new manuals reflected the modern approach to musketry, drill and fire control of Austrian, French and Swedish models.

As far as weapons were concerned, Peter had already purchased as many as 30 to 40,000 muskets in England during his visit in 1698. The import of a further 25,000 handguns between 1700 and 1710 was matched by increased indigenous production in the same decade – from a mere 6,000 in 1701 to 30,000 a year in 1706 and 40,000 in 1711. This was made possible by the burgeoning development of the Urals iron industry. By 1725 Russia was practically self-sufficient in iron. Plug bayonets were replacing the obsolescent pikes in the West in the 1690s and early 1700s. The new flintlock, already standard in these countries in 1700, soon found its way into Peter's army, but there was a significant modification – the new ring bayonet in place of its 'plug' counterpart enabled the infantryman to fire with bayonet attached, thus making him more flexible, especially in attack.

Reform of the cavalry was slow and least effective. Dragoons* were raised in 1701, but the basic problem of command and control was never fully resolved. After a disastrous defeat at Mur (1705), Peter commented, 'Many times have I spoken about the insufficient training of the dragoons' [48 *p. 58–9*]. Nevertheless, as the years passed, discipline improved under Menshikov's expert eye, and a special light corps of cavalry known as the *corvolant** – an amalgam of cavalry, light infantry and light artillery – came into being. Changes in cavalry tactics and discipline were important, but Geoffrey Parker has shown that it was experience, the percentage of veterans present, that so often held the key to success [70 *p. 24*].

Changes in artillery were more effective. Though Russian siege guns had acquired a good reputation, the disaster of Narva showed them to be obsolete. Peter set a Russian-born Dutchman, Andrew Vinius, to update this arm. As with the handguns, Peter's fast-developing heavy-iron industry in the Urals was essential. Indeed, by 1705 the rapid expansion in the Urals led the English ambassador to report that the artillery was 'as at present extremely well-served' [48 *p. 59*]. When the Russians captured Narva in 1704, their veteran Scottish commander, George Ogilvie, was able to comment that he had never seen a nation 'go better to work with their cannons and mortars' [48 *p. 59*]. By 1709 there were new types of light artillery, with three-pounders being used in support of the infantry.

THE NAVY

Far more revolutionary, however, was the creation of the navy in the face of bitter hostility and against all the odds. Russians had no love for the sea, but Peter himself was so obsessional about it that he became personally and emotionally involved in the enterprise [*Doc. 3*]. He was driven on by his determination to challenge Swedish naval predominance in the Baltic which made Russian naval expansion imperative.

This had already been prefigured in the 1660s and, as we have seen in chapter one, Peter started a shipbuilding plan for the Azov adventure. Barges and galleys, as well as two large 36-gun ships, had been built at Voronezh, but their quality was far from adequate. As with the army, Peter now ordered his subjects to contribute to the navy. The church and secular landowners had to supply one ship per 8,000 peasant households, while merchants as a class had to provide twelve, later fourteen, vessels.

As a result of these measures, by 1698 there was a Black Sea fleet of 50 ships. For the Baltic, shipbuilding started in earnest at Ladeinoe Pole on the river Svir. In November 1704 it also began at St Petersburg's new Admiralty complex. The first ship for the Baltic was launched in August 1703, followed in 1704 by six frigates* and many galleys. Ships-of-the-line, each by definition with at least 60 guns, followed – 10 in 1710, 17 in 1714 and 32 in 1724. In the Baltic, however, it was galleys that counted, and here Peter sought to outstrip the Swedes, who had allowed their victorious galley fleet to decline to the benefit of ships-of-the-line. The shallow-draft galleys were ideal for supporting landforces on Swedish and Finnish coastlines, yet by 1710 Russia had 100 galleys, Sweden only 5. At the Battle of Hangö Udd (Cape Hangö) in 1714 Russia had 20 ships-of-the-line and 200 galleys. Not surprisingly, naval expenditure rose sharply – 81,000 roubles in 1701, 204,000 in 1706, 700,000 in 1715 and 1,200,000 in 1724. By 1725 Peter's

Baltic fleet, with 34 ships-of-the-line, 15 frigates, numerous galleys and 28,000 men, was larger than any other in the Baltic [*Doc. 20*]. Though in the West the Dutch were preeminent in shipbuilding, it was English shipwrights who predominated in Russia. Of the 34 Russian Baltic ships-of-the-line, 20 were English-built. In fact, in July 1719 Russian naval power was growing so rapidly that the British ambassador tried to persuade English shipwrights to go home.

Depending as it did on gunnery, seamanship and navigation, naval training was bound to be technical. Skilled manpower initially was scarce, and Peter sought to redress this by expanding training. In 1698 he founded a navigation school at Azov and three years later did the same at Moscow. This was followed by the setting-up of a naval academy at St Petersburg which by 1718 had 500 students (see pages 83–4). Most sailors were perforce recruited from former soldiers and inland boatmen, but Peter also had to rely heavily on foreigners. Most of the 1,000 westerners he brought back from the Great Embassy were assigned for service in the navy. As with the army and industry, he also sent young potential naval officers to the West to serve in the French, Dutch and Venetian fleets. Several served in the British navy, among them Apraksin's own nephew, who served for seven years from 1709 to 1716.

Though Peter made Russia potentially one of the great naval powers of Europe, especially in the Baltic, we must be careful not to overestimate the impact he made during his lifetime. It is true that in 1696 his new galleys helped to capture Azov, in 1714 were decisive at Hangö Udd and again in raids on the Swedish coast in 1719–20, but his larger, more prestigious ships-of-the-line were rarely of much use. The new Azov fleet achieved nothing, and in any case had to be destroyed after the Peace of Pruth (1711). The Baltic fleet only took one enemy ship-of-the-line in the whole Northern War, while the Danish fleet captured four in one year (1715). Unpopular heavy expenditure and the 'peace dividend' after Nystad led to a rapid decline, which became precipitous after 1725, so that the fleet barely survived. It was left to Catherine II later in the century to develop what Peter had begun.

The increase in military and naval strength was probably the most far-reaching achievement of Peter's reign. The spectacular modernisation, reform and enlargement of the armed forces not only protected Russia at a moment of grave danger, but in the long term gave her real prestige and respect in Europe that was to last two centuries. Russia was no longer a ripe fruit, ready for picking, but a nation to be admired, or at least respected. She administered a cataclysmic shock to Sweden in 1709 and 1714, and her subsequent aggressive posturing and expansionism became a matter of major concern not only to the traditional Baltic powers, but also to Britain, newly associated with Hanover.

6 THE RUSSIAN ECONOMY

The rapid and sudden growth in the economy during Peter's reign was remarkable. There is little doubt that Peter's motivation, at least up to about 1709, was to supply the needs of his greatly enlarged army and navy, but the repercussions spread wide and deep, particularly in the uppermost sections of society. Above all, as Matthew Anderson [38 *p. 98*] has written, Peter's aim, rooted in his own personality, was not merely to copy the West but to induce in Russia a new spirit of work, enterprise and efficiency, to enable its thinly spread population to tap the country's vast natural resources. Hence his stress on the need for duty, work and achievement.

The assessment of late nineteenth-century Russian historians that Peter's economic policy was revolutionary has since been revised. Current historians see his reign as part of a long-term economic development, though at the same time recognising Peter's particular dynamism and charisma. Nor is it any longer thought to have been a 'hothouse' development, rootless and therefore short-lived. Modern research, both in the former Soviet Union and in the United States, shows that it was sufficiently rooted to continue, despite the less dynamic characters of Peter's successors [51]. He had propelled Russia onto the world stage and they felt bound to keep the machine going. Industrial development centred mainly on iron and copper, textiles, small arms and cannon, sulphur, gunpowder and paper. During Peter's reign 86 factories were established for these purposes. Most significant of all, however, was the massive rise in iron production from 120,000–150,000 poods* (a pood = 36 lbs) in 1700 to 1,165,000 by the time of his death in 1725 – a tenfold increase overall. Connected with the metallurgical industries was the development of small arms manufacture. To meet the army's demand in 1711 for 122,600 muskets for the infantry and 49,800 for the cavalry, production was increased at existing sites, at Tula, just over 100 miles south of Moscow, and Olonets, in the north of Russia. The first state-run textile factories to provide uniforms for the army were established at Voronezh in 1704 and at Moscow in 1705.

With these industrial needs in mind, Peter aimed to enlist private funds and initiative. His objective, drawn from experience in The Netherlands and England, was to create, where possible, a class of entrepreneurs who would use the incentive of market forces to innovate and build up capital. The decrees of 1711 make this abundantly clear. They allowed people of all ranks to trade in any commodity anywhere, and put an end to most state monopolies and state control. For example, restrictions on the production of salt, tobacco, talc and bristles were abolished, so that after 1719 only two state monopolies, those on potash and resin, remained.

Despite Peter's desire to encourage private initiative, so rudimentary was independent commercial and industrial life that state involvement was imperative. The government was to be the teacher and guardian of this new class of entrepreneurs. In order to fulfil Peter's aim of 'manufacturing the manufacturers', state enterprise was to be the guiding light [51 *p. 38*]. There are a number of examples of this educative attitude: one is the issue of detailed instructions on the curing of leather with ram oil instead of pitch. To increase productivity in the textile industry Peter encouraged methods of weaving broader woollen cloth, while in agriculture he advocated the use of the scythe in place of the inefficient sickle. Seeking for skilled advisers to direct overall reform, Peter went to great lengths to try and entice to his service the Scottish financier, John Law, famed throughout Europe for his achievement in establishing a national bank in France. Yet even the offer of a princely title, the ownership of 2,000 peasant households and the right to build a new town, to fill it with foreign artisans and thus further bolster the economy, all failed to capture him. After 1714 Peter made use of advisers closer to home, such as the Saxon baron, Ludwig Luberas, Count Savva Raguzinskii, Peter S. Saltykov and others. In addition, he established the Business College in 1718, the College of Mines (*berg kollegiya**) in 1719 and the College of Manufactures (*kommerts-kollegiya*) in 1723. Furthermore, it is clear from the decrees written in his own hand that Peter involved himself personally and with considerable intensity in every aspect of his reform programme, seeing it as his duty as tsar not merely to reinforce Russia militarily and economically, but also to better the lot of his people.

BARRIERS TO PROGRESS

The communication problem was the most obvious brake on Peter's economic plans, though by upgrading existing roads, building new ones and developing a canal system he did much to overcome it. The most notable road development was from Moscow to St Petersburg, following an 825 kilometre route surveyed by Farquharson in 1712. Its original tree-trunk foundation was prone to rot and consequently return to natural marsh, but with later improvements between 1725 and 1760 it cut the journey time from five weeks to two.

The poor river system in the St Petersburg hinterland near Lake Ladoga, itself subject to wild storms, was improved with the aid of foreign engineers, such as John Perry, a disciple of Newton and recruited in London in 1698, who set about canalising the rivers and building new canals between them [*Doc. 37*]. Peter ordered the construction of a coherent canal system to cover the 100 miles between the Don and Volga and Oka. After ten years' hard labour, however, the loss of Azov (1711) left this grand design unfinished, so he turned his attention to upgrading communications with his newly acquired Baltic provinces. Already in 1709 the Neva and the Volga had been connected by a canal, built by Dutch engineers, through which more than 2,000 tons of freight passed each year between 1712 and 1719. The bypass round the stormy Lake Ladoga was started in 1718, but not finished until 1732. Despite all these measures, however, it was not until nineteenth-century railway development that the problem of transportation over such great distances was finally solved.

Another problem was the inertia and innate conservatism of the Russian people, in spite of the impetus given by Peter himself after his own visit to the West [*Docs. 18* and *19*]. The very institution of serfdom tended to make the lords (*pomeshchiki* *) indolent and therefore conservative. Consequently Peter had to resort to duress. For instance, in an edict of 1723 he observed that 'Either our decrees are not accurately observed or there are few people who wish to go into the business of manufacturing ...; ... in manufacturing affairs we must not be satisfied with the proposition only, but we must act and even compel, and help [people] by teaching, by machines and other aids, and even by compulsion to become good economists ...' [*48 p. 162–3*].

Yet another problem was a shortage of both capital and labour. The merchant class remained so embryonic that even at the end of Peter's reign, despite all his massive efforts at liberalisation, albeit under governmental paternalism, the state still controlled much of the economy. For instance, of the 31 iron metalworks in the Urals, 15 were still state-run in 1725. The government also established about half of the 178 'factories' created in Peter's reign. For various reasons many foundered before they could fully develop. Strong foreign competition was one factor, which Peter tried to combat with his Tariff of 1724. But there was also a lack of skilled labour and, of course, a limited domestic market in a basically peasant country whose needs were supplied by handicraft industries. Even at the end of the century Russia was still primarily an exporter of raw materials and semi-finished goods and a net importer of industrial products.

In a desperate attempt to remedy the situation, Peter prodigally used government finance to induce private owners to involve themselves ever more heavily in industry. He spent as much as 8 to 10 per cent, sometimes even 20 per cent, of his revenue in encouraging manufacturing. At other times government assistance took the form of interest-free loans or subsidies, both to individuals and to companies. The Tariff of 1724 which heavily restricted imports was also intended to encourage private economic growth. Despite all this, enthusiasm for entrepreneurship remained at best limited. Peter's *ukaz* of 1712, which aimed at the creation of companies of merchants to establish textile factories, met with hostility from, of all people, the merchants themselves, partly because Peter underestimated the differences in risk and investment returns between Western Europe and Russia, and partly because politically he 'considered himself the guardian of the welfare of his subjects', even of entrepreneurs [54 and 51 *p. 66*]. In any case, at this stage the embryonic group of entrepreneurs was still 'willing to operate under an umbrella of basically paternalistic and pro-tectionist government policies' [54 and 51 *p. 67*].

Some historians, such as Madame E.V. Spiridonova [cited in 38 *p. 191*], have maintained that Peter tried to copy Western mercantilism*, but in Simone Blanc's view, Peter and his principal economic advisers, Ordin-Nashchokin and Pososhkov, far from being dogmatic followers of Colbertian mercantilism, were merely recognising that infant Russian industry needed protection to survive 'for the same evident reason that two men, one in Europe and one in Asia, go under the sun to warm up and under the shade to cool off' [51 *p. 31*].

Though Peter never used foreign capital, he was prepared to bolster industry by using foreign technical specialists, such as

German miners, Italian silk workers, British engineers like Perry and Farquharson [*Doc. 5*], and Dutch mining experts, like Henning. Indeed they were vital to his plans, but even here some of the best were not really foreign, since they had already been Russianised. For instance, James Bruce, of Scottish stock, at first employed in industry but later as a diplomat at Nystad (May 1721), had been born and bred in Russia. Some of these foreigners were involved in management, but far more were employed in the specialist, technical field where they were most significant. The great majority of skilled and unskilled workers at a lower level were totally Russian, working in small-scale 'shops' or at home.

Nevertheless Peter's industrial policy did have its success. By 1726 52 per cent of Russia's exports were simple manufactured goods, mainly linen, canvas and iron. Some of the firms were of colossal size for the time; the sailcloth factory in Moscow, for instance, employing 1,162 workers, was by far the largest in Europe [38 *p. 102*]. Peter had hoped to develop a large-scale textile industry, principally for making military and naval uniforms, thus ensuring Russian independence of imports. But although a textile industry certainly got under way, it was not on a sufficient scale. By the end of the reign, woollen cloth was still being imported from Yorkshire and its rivals, Prussia and Silesia, though the lining (*karazeia*) was wholly Russian.

THE IRON INDUSTRY

The flagship of industrial growth was at all times the burgeoning new metal industry of the Urals, where great quantities of both iron and copper had been discovered. As we have seen, in 1631 Vinius the elder founded a factory at Tula, where in the 1620s high quality iron ore had been discovered on the River Upa, 112 miles south of Moscow. Another was established at Olonets in the north, not far from the future St Petersburg. Nevertheless, at the beginning of Peter's reign there were still only 17 ironworks of any size in Muscovy. Existing sources of raw material were insufficient, especially in view of the army's desperate need for more metal. Peter's discovery of iron in the Urals had a seismic effect, even though it was 1,000 miles away from the centres of population. Close by were all the ingredients for rapid development – ample waterpower from the mountains, an immense supply of charcoal from the forests and, once forced migration had taken place, cheap labour. Peter set up the first foundry in that area at Nevyansk in

1699. From then onwards expansion was unceasing almost until Peter's death in 1725, when there were 52 ironworks in Muscovy, of which 13, with their larger furnaces and better equipment, were in the Urals. However, the difficulties caused by the great distance of the Urals iron industry from the chief centres of population and administration remained, for it took two navigational seasons to bring a load from the Volga to St Petersburg.

Almost inevitably, the main impetus for iron production came from the state. By the late 1690s the government, with the close involvement of Peter himself, had developed large state foundries. This development was supervised by Andrei A. Vinius, coincidentally head of the *Sibirskii prikaz* and the Russo-Dutch son of Vinius the elder, founder of Tula. Later, towards the end of Peter's reign, the whole state-run iron and copper enterprise in the Urals was in the hands of Henning, a Dutchman whom Peter had recruited during the Great Embassy in the 1690s. By the 1720s, thanks to Henning, the Urals state industry was supplying 20 per cent of the whole Russian production.

Though the bulk of iron production remained under government control, the private sector was certainly far from insignificant; in the Urals it accounted for another 20 per cent. The rise of the metal industry had its social impact on the entrepreneur class, some of whom rapidly rose from rags to riches. The most remarkable example was an illiterate worker from Tula, Nikita Demidov, who after amassing large sums in Tula was given, in 1702, the principal responsibility for developing the Urals. Peter challenged him to emulate the Germans, and he did. The most active foundry builder in the years after 1716, Demidov was undoubtedly the greatest industrialist in Russia. Peter acknowledged this in 1720 by granting him noble status, made hereditary five years later. By 1762 the Demidov family owned 28 ironworks of different kinds, and this newly established dynasty was still operating on a large scale in the 1850s.

The rapid discovery of rich new veins of iron ore and other metals and the massive movement of skilled and ascribed labour* led to particularly rapid expansion between 1699 and 1703. During these years the first copper foundry was established, again under government initiative, to respond to the growing demands of the Moscow and St Petersburg mints. The Urals not only had a virtual monopoly of copper production; the region also remained the leader of the heavy metal industry until the rise of south-Russian iron production in the 1860s. This was one of Peter's major bequests to

Russia, for it soon began to make its impact on Europe. Russian iron of high quality was already emerging on the London market by 1716 [*Doc. 21*]. By the middle of the eighteenth century Russia was outproducing Britain, whose historic Sussex ironfields, denuded of forests, had run short of charcoal. Russia furthermore soon outstripped Sweden as the leading European producer of iron and became the largest exporter to England. It was not until the end of the century that England regained the lead with the discovery of coke smelting, with which Russia could not compete.

It has already been noted that the nineteenth-century view of Peter's industrial developments as a flimsily rooted growth which withered abruptly after 1725 is no longer held. Despite the impact of his death (1725), as well as the end of the Great Northern War (1721) and of the campaign against Persia (1724), there was very little, if any, decline in industrial activity. As many as 86 per cent of private ironworks survived beyond 1745, along with 72 per cent of textile works. The entrepreneurial class, already emerging strongly under Peter, came into their own after his death, and the dip in governmental activity was more than matched by the increase in the private sector [51 *p. 59–60*]. Trade with Britain increased and copper output doubled in the years 1725–27 [51 *p. 60*] [*Doc. 21*]. Previous historians owe their misconception regarding the lack of Russian entrepreneurial spirit to the propaganda of Peter's own writings [54 cited in 51 *p. 66*] which in turn were based on his own misunderstanding of the situation.

LABOUR

Vast industrial undertakings, especially in the iron and construction industries, demanded an equally vast workforce. Geographically, this was especially significant in the two new principal areas of activity, St Petersburg and the Urals, which were both previously thinly populated. By 1725 there were 30,000 ascribed peasants in the Urals ironworking region, which effectively doubled its population within twenty years. This required a rigorous regime of employment, mostly using forced labour. In common with contemporary west European practice, Peter often used soldiers.

Besides army and navy recruits, there was also the great pool of criminals and vagrants who were often pressed into service, and the purely Russian phenomenon of ascribed labour, first used in the mid-seventeenth century, but vastly extended by Peter. By 1719 31,000 men had been ascribed, rising to 54,000 in 1725 for such great enterprises as the construction of the wharves at Voronezh (1699–1701, 20,000 workers were used), Taganrog (1701, 9,000 workers), the Volga-Don canals (1698, 20,000 workers) and St Petersburg itself (1709 onwards, where 40,000 workers were used). In 1721, there were 15,000 army recruits working on the canals generally and 20,000 by 1724. In fact, as was commonly the case, Peter rarely managed to raise more than one-quarter or one-third of the numbers he intended for St Petersburg. Even these were often dispersed on other schemes, such as 12,000 for the southern fortresses being constructed against the everpresent Turkish threat. St Petersburg's Admiralty building, the largest single project, absorbed 1,626 labourers a year. Others were used in shipyards and supporting factories.

Recruitment on this scale, despite the abandonment of Taganrog and the Volga-Don canal, showed that the Petrine administration could galvanise the nation into work, even if some people slipped through the net. Skilled workers were moved forcibly with their whole families to be settled for life in St Petersburg, the first group arriving from Olonets in 1705. By 1712 two-thirds of St Petersburg's workforce were forced labourers, many from the 24,000 peasant households in the St Petersburg and Archangel districts. They were taken in units of 3,300 at a time, and were required to work for four-month periods. The remaining third were free labourers who, though more efficient, were costly. Life as a conscript worker was tough, even by the standards of the period. The working day was between eleven and a half and thirteen hours long, depending on the season, though this regime was leavened by free time on Sundays and the 44 saints' days. Accommodation was either nonexistent, in the summer, or in the form of primitive tents and dugouts. Such conditions were inevitably harmful to health and efficiency. In 1716, for example, 1,000 of the 32,000 men working in St Petersburg died and a further 1,000 were seriously ill. The very existence of the armed forces and workers in such a barren northern climate created a demand for a support force to supply food and other necessities. Though this was an ancillary service, it became an immense undertaking, carried out mainly by workers from monastic lands in north and central Russia. In 1702, for instance, these gangs carried 4,428 cartloads of bread and 8,593 loads of war supplies. In the following year the figures rose to 5,290 and 11,318 respectively, as building increased.

The natural unpopularity of forced labour and army recruitment led to a high degree of defection, usually to the vast steppe areas south of the river Don. The only way to ensure the safe arrival of workers for St Petersburg was to provide an armed guard, sometimes as many as one to each eight or nine conscripts, who were brought in chains almost as convicts. The loss of labour from the land was equally unpopular among the landlords. Because Peter's sympathies lay rather with the merchant-industrialists and their desperate need, in 1721 he gave them special rights to purchase serfs or whole villages for attachment to the factory itself and not to the factory owner. However, hostility from landowners rendered this decree largely inoperative, though it remained in force until 1762.

AGRICULTURE

Despite massive industrial development, agriculture was still the occupation of most Russians, but the harsh climate and, in the Moscow area, the poor soil made any improvement difficult. One twentieth-century economic historian has written that so great was Moscow's infertility that if there had been significant economic growth in that region there would have been very speedy overpopulation and destitution [50 in 51 *p. 9*]. It was not until the absorption of the rich, naturally fertile, black soil of the Ukraine and the Hungarian plain that Russian agricultural production could advance. A census taken nineteen years after Peter's death showed that the steepest percentage increases in population had occurred not in Russia itself, but in the border areas, the lower Volga, the Urals and the Ukraine. As Jeremy Black suggests, for Russia the development of steppe lands for supplies of food was as important as the conquest of the Swedish Baltic provinces [17 *p. 25*].

A number of Russian nobles in the 1700s were increasingly interested in efficient estate management, as exemplified in the *Instructions* for one of the Sheremetiev estates in 1703. Record keeping, improvement of yields and the organisation of rent obligations all demonstrated the same keenness in proper management. Developments thus set in motion led to a vast increase in grain production in the second quarter of the century. This, coupled with the completion of the new transport canal system linking St Petersburg and the Volga, led to a drop in grain prices in St Petersburg and a consequent rise in the standard of living. Indeed, the rise in grain production kept pace with the growth in population in the 1740s and 1750s so that there was a sizeable surplus for export to Europe. In this way Peter's transport improvements bore fruit.

CONCLUSION

Peter regulated trade far more than any of his predecessors, especially through the College of Commerce after 1718 and the protectionist Tariff of 1724. He also strove to dominate the Ukrainian economy for the benefit of Russia. From 1714 Ukrainian trade was compulsorily channelled through Russian ports, and in 1719 Ukrainians were forbidden to export their valuable wheat, since a lower price benefited Russia.

Economically Peter did not achieve all he set out to do, and historians have criticised him for an overprotectionist trade policy and – incorrectly as we have seen – for the hothouse rapidity of his factory programme. Nevertheless, he did inspire the Russian economy with a new impetus and a new direction, laying the foundations for future growth under Elizabeth and Catherine. He gave Russia one new port and capital, St Petersburg, and he acquired another, better, natural port, Riga; he also began the canal network which was later to play such a vital part in Russian industrial and commercial growth.

7 ADMINISTRATIVE REFORMS

EXISTING INSTITUTIONS AND THE NEED FOR CHANGE

Statebuilding, such as Peter was engaged in, required not only accession of territory abroad, but also assertion of sovereignty at home. The vast area of Russia had hitherto been governed at the centre by a mere 2,000 men, apart from scribes. The cumbrous, inefficient machinery of government, like early medieval western administration, was mostly unspecialised. At Peter's accession there were as many as 44 departments, or *prikazy*, with little differentiation in function [*Doc. 22*]. Most, like the *Sibirskii prikaz* which supervised Siberia, were omnicompetent for particular geographical areas. Others, such as the *posolskii prikaz*, the foreign affairs department, were more specialised. There were even some, particularly those associated with tax collection, which were a relic of the days of Mongol occupation. Russia, it could be said, had a multitude of institutions, but no coherent constitution. The consequent logjam, inertia and inefficiency made it ripe for reform. Early in his reign Peter had a real chance of grappling with this particular problem, because one close friend, Feodor A. Golovin, controlled as many as six *prikazy*, but preoccupation with the war and Golovin's premature death at 55 in 1706, meant that the chance was missed.

Furthermore, since the Romanovs' accession to power in 1613, the Council of *Boyars*, the *Boyarskaya Duma*, had lost its useful function as an adminstrative assembly of magnates. The inner circle of 20 or 30 families of ancient lineage remained, and though it had been strengthened by Alexis's infusion of *parvenus* with specialised skills after 1645, members newly created in the 1670s and 1680s were mostly court favourites of little value. Though the *Duma's* nominal membership declined in the 1690s from 182 to 86, only 30 or 40 actually attended and these had little influence.

Until 1709, preoccupation with Turkey and Sweden kept Peter's attention from coherent administrative reform. Changes were *ad hoc*, spasmodic and directed to the prosecution of the war – recruitment and provision of weaponry, ammunition, food and communications for his troops. Indeed, the very addition of *ad hoc* departments under stress of war itself added to the confusion. As one historian has put it, at best Peter could only approach the problem as an artificer rather than an architect [48 *p. 123*].

Peter's awareness of his absolute power was matched by determination to exercise this power for the good of all. In a speech made in the Troitskii Cathedral on 22 October 1721 he declared that he would 'labour for the general benefit and profit' [34 *p. 30*]. Though earlier Muscovite rulers might have shown concern for the welfare of their subjects, none was ever a 'ubiquitous mentor' [48 *p. 123*]. However, Peter, though well intentioned, was intrusive. He targeted the minutiae of private life, such as clothing, appearance, conduct in church and the width of the cloth his people wove. He issued decrees on house design and chimneys; roofs were to be Ukrainian in style, of tiles, sod or shingles, not boards or lathes. Plaster ceilings were to replace traditional exposed timberwork. Other decrees dealt with shoe manufacture, the use of the scythe instead of the sickle which we have already noted (spring 1721) and the annotation of textbooks (1723). There were to be no rowing boats on the Neva, only sailing ones – and even these had to be copied from a new design, the *kolomenka*, on pain of a lifetime in the galleys (1718). For the land-loving Russians there was to be regular sailing practice on Sundays. But through it all, tough though he was, Peter showed a profound sense of the common good; and whereas pre-Petrine legislation had been based on fear, Peter's was grounded on reasoned explanation. The frequency of decrees intensified from 36 a year in the late seventeenth century to 160 in the first half of the eighteenth. Of the published legislation and regulation of Peter's reign, 70 per cent was concerned with control over his subjects' lives in one way or another.

THE SENATE

The creation of the Senate, Peter's first serious attempt at administrative reform, was itself an answer to the exigencies of war. Set up temporarily in February 1711 as a body of nine officials to act in his absence on the Pruth campaign, it had unbridled authority, unlike the Muscovite *Duma* which only acted in the tsar's presence. Subjects were ordered to submit to the senate 'as to Us Ourselves'. In 1718 Peter unwisely extended membership to presidents of all the *kollegii*, but in 1722, realising his mistake, he confined it to those of war, navy and foreign affairs. At first temporary, the Senate soon became permanent, and as well as overseeing the provinces and supervising tax collecting, it also functioned as a supreme law court. Its legislative power, in fact little used, was taken away in 1721 at the end of the Northern War. The decrees which established it in 1711 were followed by others, designating different senators for duty each day (1714) and prescribing the frequency of meetings – three a week in 1716, raised to four or five in 1718. Regulations regarding the actual meetings were strict. There was a fine of 50 roubles for non-attendance and further fines (or even imprisonment) for idle conversation. Nevertheless, the Senate was not without faults. Two of the original senators were convicted of peculation, knouted,* maimed, and suffered forfeiture of their property. The Senate was also overloaded. On one day, 10 November 1721, the following items appeared on the agenda – a school for civil servants, the governorship of Kazan, the Table of Ranks, canals, the road to Moscow, supervision of *voevody*, supplies for the Admiralty and the marking of trees. Little wonder that in its appellate capacity the Senate only heard an average of one case a year. Furthermore, senators were soon in conflict with the provincial governors. Recent research by Brenda Meehan-Waters and others shows that Peter intended senatorship as an active post, not as a mark of distinction in old age or a reward for past service [80]. Senators were meant to be people in the prime of life and capable of vigorous work. In fact, half of those appointed for the first time were under 50, and even after the establishment of the Table of Ranks they were superior to it and thus had no such rank entitlement, or *chin*,* attached to them. Membership of the Ranks was indeed lowly compared with senatorship. 'It was a heady thing to be a Petrine senator' [80 *p. 102*].

In 1715, to oversee the Senate's often unruly sessions Peter appointed his tutor's son, Vasily I. Zotov, with the title of Inspector General. Three years later he abolished this post, and experimented unsuccessfully with a chief secretary and with guards officers, before appointing a *Generalprokuror** who was to be 'the tsar's eye and personal representative in state affairs' [74 *p. 91*]. This new official had a threefold task. First, though not a senator himself, he presided over meetings in Peter's absence. Second, he had a new team of procurators to watch over each of the colleges; and third, as *oberfiskal*,* he masterminded the secret work of the 500 detested *fiskaly,** originally appointed in 1711 to seek out corruption and mismanagement at all levels. They had a financial incentive to investigate and accuse officials of whatever seniority, even senators. As one recent writer has put it, 'it was difficult to answer that all-important question so succinctly put by Lenin, who dominates whom?' [21 *p. 82*]. The *Generalprokuror* was in all but name deputy tsar. The first was Pavel Yaguzhinzkii, like Menshikov of humble birth and yet his ruthless, hated rival. Though energetic, decisive and loyal, he lacked the administrative capacity necessary for such a vital post at a time of rapid reform.

COLLEGES

The Senate lasted for another two centuries as a supreme lawcourt and formulator of policy, but its inefficiency led Peter to experiment with the system of administrative colleges, *kollegii*, partly prefigured in the specialisation of some *prikazys*' work in 1699–1701; the *Preobrazhenskii prikaz,** for instance, was to search out disruptive elements, and the admiralty *prikaz* to oversee shipbuilding. The college system, new to Russia, was borrowed from the West. Peter took advice in England from the 'pious and learned Francis Lee M.D.' (1698) [21 *p. 83*] and in Prussia from Leibniz (1712), who likened its mechanism to 'that of watches, whose wheels mutually keep each other in movement' [48 *p. 126*]. However, his main collaborators after 1714 were Heinrich Fick, a former Swedish civil servant, originally from Hamburg, and Johann Luberas, a Silesian baron, who presented him with a survey of European administrative systems. After finding England's system of commissions too unsystematic and Holland's too decentralised, Peter and his advisers chose Sweden's, with its 'closed and unitary character' [82 *p. 416*], as their model for an effective central administration.

Inspired by the survey, Peter sent Fick back to Stockholm surreptitiously to collect copies of Swedish administrative legislation, while Luberas journeyed to western Europe to recruit 150 personnel. Though Peter himself worked on the proposed constitutions with his usual intensity (in the twelve drafts there are corrections in his own hand), recent work by the Swedish legal historian, Claes Peterson, shows Fick's role, often underrated by Soviet historians, to have been vital [82] [*Docs. 23* and *25*]. Peter rewarded him with an Estonian estate and appointment as economic adviser (1724). By 1717 the new scheme was ready to go into operation.

Instead of the 44 *prikazy* there were now to be eleven colleges, three of which – foreign affairs, war and admiralty, (*kollegiya inostrannykh del, krigs kollegiya, admiralteiskaya kollegiya*) – created in 1718 [21 p. 83], were to take precedence over the others. Of the remainder, three – *kamer-kollegiya, shtats-kontor-kollegiya* and *revision kollegiya* – dealt with finance; three – *berg-kollegiya, manufaktur-kollegiya* and *kommerts-kollegiya* – with industrial and commercial life; one – *yustits-kollegiya* – with justice and provincial government, and the eleventh – *vochinnaya-kollegiya*, established in 1721 – with questions regarding land. Oversight of the colleges was in the hands of the *Generalprokuror* and the Senate. Each college was finely regulated, with a fixed establishment of eleven – a president, a vice-president, a foreign adviser, four counsellors and four assessors – apart from clerks and translators, who were either Luberas's recruits from the West or Swedish prisoners-of-war. Meeting in impressive surroundings, the colleges worked by majority voting under the *fiskals'* watchful eyes. By 1722, however, most foreigners had been discharged, and this left the presidents vying with each other for power much as the old *prikazy* had done, and corruption returned despite Fick's advice on salaries [*Doc. 25*] and Peter's creation of the new post of *reketmeister** specifically to hear complaints. By the end of the reign, government was almost as cumbrous as it had been at the beginning.

However, despite their later decline the colleges were an improvement on the *prikazy*. Freed from detailed administration, the Senate, too, was effective in policy making, in preparing legislation, and carrying out judicial functions in its appellate capacity; the routine judicial work with which it formerly dealt had been largely taken over by the *yustits-kollegiya*.

LOCAL GOVERNMENT

Peter made some impact on local, as well as central, government. Because Muscovite local government under *voevody* was unable to cope with the additional strains put on it in time of war, Peter embarked on a series of confusing and often ill-judged reforms in which he too often ignored the human factor. In December 1708 he divided Russia into eight vast governorships (*gubernii**) whose main responsibility was revenue collection and recruitment; the number was subsequently increased to ten, then in 1718 to twelve. The military motive was paramount. Since all the governorships except Moscow were border-territories, Peter appointed close associates as governors, with wide powers over taxation, policing and recruitment – to the detriment of the old central *prikazy* and colleges. Each of the vast governorships was subdivided into *uezdy** (districts), under a *voivod*, soon to be renamed *Kommandant*. At first provincial governors ruled alone, but in 1715 Peter introduced a system of *landrats*, or committees, of which the governor (*gubernator*) was merely to be chairman, with members – usually ex-officers – elected by local nobles. His staff of quasi-military officials had Germanic titles – *ober-komissar* (for collecting revenue), *ober-proviant* (for receiving taxation in kind), *ober-Kommandant* (for military affairs) and *landrichter* who dealt with justice.

All was confusion, as Peter resorted to one system after another. In 1715 the *uezdy* (geographical districts) were replaced by mathematically based *doli** (fractions), each with exactly 5,536 households, but with no geographical or social functions. With Fick's help Peter set about yet more reforms in 1718. Another tier on Swedish lines, the *provintsiya*, was introduced between the *goberniya* and the *dolya*. Again it was too schematic to be workable and too little adapted to Russian life. Obsessed by the need for revenue and recruitment, Peter failed to take account of the human factor, and the underlying problem therefore remained. In the event, effective local government reform had to wait for Catherine the Great's reign.

Outside Russia proper, especially in the newly acquired Baltic provinces, Peter allowed some autonomy, but the Ukraine, where separatism was always likely, was a special case. The defection of Mazepa, the Ukrainian Cossack leader, or *hetman*, to Charles XII forced Peter to increase Russian control, by billeting troops and imposing labour conscription. After Nystad, Peter enforced Russian law in the Ukraine and created a special *kollegiya* to oversee it (1722), thereby placing it under the control of the Senate. In 1754, after Peter's death, this process was carried further with the abolition of the Russo-Ukrainian border, but not until 1782 was the Ukraine finally incorporated into the Russian provincial system, where, with the Baltic provinces, it remained until 1991.

To confuse matters still further, in 1718 Peter divided Russia into military districts directly under central, not provincial, control. He did this primarily to facilitate the collection of the poll-tax* as well as conscription levies and the billeting of his army. The poll- or soul-tax, first decreed in 1718 but not finally raised until 1724, was originally designed to replace all other taxes, and to cover the increasing costs of the army. The size of military districts depended on the numbers necessary to support a military unit; 21,863 'male souls' for an infantry regiment, 60,268 for a cavalry unit. Each 'soul' had to pay 74 kopecks; peasants without lords had to pay an extra 40, townsmen an extra 50.

There was a further complication in 1719, when, in an apparently laudable, but abortive, attempt to separate justice from administration, Peter established eleven judicial districts, organised separately from the provinces and under the central justice college (*yustits-kollegiya*). In practice, however, this merely led to rivalry and conflict between officials of three competing systems – the land commissioners (*zemskiye komissar*), the *komissars* elected by the gentry, and the military officers responsible for the construction and distribution (*raskladka*) of soldiers' quarters. In short, Peter failed to create a coherent system of local government. It was not until 1775 that there was a lasting reorganisation.

Changes in town government were more durable, partly because they were less of a breach with tradition. Peter's aim was to encourage a self-reliant middle class in whom he had a special economic interest His decree of 1699 for the government of Moscow established, instead of the eight central *prikazy*, the *ratusha.** This allowed the burgesses to run their own judicial and financial affairs [*Doc. 24*]. Subsequently, the *ratusha* developed into the national treasury, receiving in the 1700s half the total revenues of the Russian state, and later into the *kamer-kollegiya*. A second decree spread the system to provincial towns. In January 1721, with Fick's help and ideas borrowed principally from Swedish, German and Baltic cities, Peter organised city dwellers into guilds, but their autonomy was only apparent. Peter tried to control them centrally through the *glavnyi magistrat,** a new college for municipal affairs (1721), but it failed. After 1725 towns once again came under the control of the local governors and the *glavnyi magistrat* was abolished. Though Peter had given towns a new administrative structure, he had failed to inspire them with new vigour.

THE *FISKALS*

By contrast with this apparent devolution, in 1711 Peter devised an additional intrusive means of central control through the Senate, using his new class of 500 fiskaly, under the *oberfiskal*, drawn from men who owed all to the ruler – namely the lower orders and foreigners. The roles of *Generalprokuror* and *oberfiskal* were now combined. As the eyes and ears of the Senate, *fiskaly* – an oppressive, often corrupt and much hated band of men – were to seek out tax evasion, theft and fraud. Corruption was rife. Even the most active and notable of the *oberfiskals*, Alexis Nesterov – a promoted slave, who had had Prince Gagarin, Governor of Siberia, hanged in 1717 for peculation – was himself convicted and broken on the wheel for the same offence. One *Generalprokuror*, Yaghuzhinskii, admitted: 'We all steal, some on a bigger scale than others' [31 *p. 381*]. So widespread was the corruption, so intrusive the oppression, that the much respected Dolgorukii is said to have warned Peter that eventually he would have no subjects left, as all, even his closest advisers, were thieving. Peter's own vigour paralleled that of the Prussian monarchs, but the vastness of Russia, coupled with the lack of an educated, honest official class, made control virtually impossible.

THE NOBILITY AND THE TABLE OF RANKS

To provide committed and competent administrators for his increasingly centralised autocracy Peter replaced the old Muscovite *mestnichestvo** system, abolished in the 1680s, with his Table of Ranks (1722), called by one writer 'the keystone of Russian absolutism' [21 *p. 87*]. Recent scholarship has shown Peter's scheme to have been less radical than historians once thought. It was certainly not hurriedly produced, like other measures. On the contrary, it was meticulously prepared. Peter's main assistant in this task was Andrew (sometimes known as Heinrich) Ostermann, a Westphalian who had been in the Russian diplomatic service since 1711 [21]. As Russian delegate at the Åland talks, he gathered information from a Prussian colleague whose house he shared. Drawing on Prussian (1699), Swedish (1696) and Danish (1699) models, and using some Russian ideas, Ostermann produced the scheme which Peter himself revised [21 *pp. 87–90*].

Published on 14 February 1722, the Table of Ranks established the concept of *chinoproizvodstvo** (uniform ranking and career development), in which each official had a service title (*chin*) and an office (*dolzhnost*). With 262 posts in three vertical hierarchies – 126 (48 per cent) for the armed forces, 94 (36 per cent) for the civil service and 42 (16 per cent) for the court – the Table was ranged in fourteen parallel grades: there had originally been one less, but Peter created a new grade just in order to avoid the unlucky number of thirteen. Peter ranked the armed services hierarchy first, the civil service second and the court third. The highest eight grades in all three became hereditary nobles. The top four, the *generaletit*,* formed the elite, and were given corresponding privileges [*Doc. 26*]. The aim was to force the aristocracy to work for the state, which was in fact a 'logical outgrowth of earlier Russian practice in harnessing the elite to state service' [*67 p. 124*].

Peter's usual determination was evident here as elsewhere. For Peter, 'any man who gets his bread for free, even if only a small amount, will not serve the state usefully; [to] live in idleness, ... according to the scriptures, is the mother of all evil' [*67 p. 118*]. All young men, noble or otherwise, had to start at the bottom and could only rise by merit. Peter himself, for instance, retained the rank of bombardier-sergeant or galley captain until he judged himself worthy of promotion. His intention was not to undermine the nobility, merely to make them work. The lowest civil servants – clerks and copyists and skilled workers – were excluded from the Table, but it did, nevertheless, produce a new professionalism in government.

Historians have been mesmerised by the radical nature of Peter's decrees, but in fact the *boyars* had a disproportionate number of top offices, not through favouritism but because of their remarkable adaptability. They showed, in the words of Brenda Meehan-Waters, that 'the "old dogs" survived by learning "new tricks" ' [*80 p. 94*]. Western research has shown that there was less 'new blood' in the new intake than used to be thought, less indeed than in Sweden, despite Menshikov's personal aversion for the old nobility [*80*]. Peter, who held similar views, had to temporise. Provincial governors, who at first in 1708 were noble with the notable exception of Menshikov, remained outside the Table of Ranks when it was established. The hereditary nobility or churchmen had no place *ex officio* in the Ranks, but, though Peter was attracted to the concept of meritocracy, even he found he had to turn to the nobility for leadership. He 'instinctively accepted the high nobility's claim to leadership, but insisted that the sons and grandsons of the *boyars* of the seventeenth century undergo rigorous training for modern warfare' [*77 p. 166*]. Thus they retained their traditional position as the tsar's leading advisers by learning to manipulate the new bureaucratic machine.

The old Muscovite title of *boyar*, last granted in 1709 to Feodor M. Apraksin, was replaced by new Western titles, such as count and baron and privy councillor. Even so, service became the only criterion for promotion. Unlike the West, where the nobility increasingly lost influence, compulsory involvement of the nobility in government became a feature not only of Russia and Prussia but of eastern European absolutism in general. In the Russian army, for instance, by 1720–21 61.9 per cent of officers were noble by birth. Of the 316 who had risen from the ranks hardly any reached higher than subaltern, only 20 became captain and only one lieutenant-colonel. It is perhaps not surprising to find the highest proportion of those of non-noble birth (18 out of 56) in Peter's own guards regiments.

Nobles may have dominated the bureaucracy, but the bureaucracy also dominated them. A lifetime's commitment away from their estates could be distasteful, onerous and expensive. Half of the elite officials (*generaletit*) died in office; some retired only to be recalled. Archives are full of letters from nobles wearily asking for permission to retire to their home estates. Divorced from their localities, the landowning class became national and bureaucratic rather than local. Although the nobles retained much of their power and influence, the Table of Ranks eroded their monopoly by enabling non-nobles and foreigners to reach parity with them. According to one study, foreigners occupied 30 per cent of the posts in the *generaletit*. Presidency of colleges was forbidden to them, though one Moscow-born Scot, Iakov Vilimovich Brus (James Bruce), did achieve that office.

Because work in the administration demanded education, Peter decreed in 1714 that all noble children between ten and fifteen should have training in mathematics, geometry and grammar. The guards regiments had an essential role in this. Peter insisted that all nobles should have training or do service in the guards, and in 1714 made guards' service a prerequisite for nobles' promotion to officer rank. Thirty-three per cent of the elite of 1730 had started in the guards, 41 per cent had served in them at some time. Entry to the guards thus became popular and therefore competitive.

Mobility between military and civil hierarchies became commonplace, so that 78 per cent of the *generaletit* had had mixed service. *Boyars* and princes, desiring to emulate Peter's own devotion to military success, coveted general rank. Of the *generaletit* in 1730, 67 per cent held military titles, but only after long service, for it took twenty years on average to move from the sixth to the second rank. 'Military uniforms permanently replaced the gold-threaded robes of Muscovy. It was a mandarin's nightmare and a field-marshal's dreamland' [80 *p. 89*].

So strong was the military ethos that by 1725 Peter's rule had come to resemble a military occupation. Military dress was widespread and even senior officials often lived in fear of junior guards officers, the *apparachiks* of the regime. As one recent historian has put it, Peter 'created not the "well-ordered police state" of early eighteenth-century cameralist philosophy, but a pettifogging and brutal despotism which perpetuated old abuses under a veneer of European terminology' [*55 p. 135*].

8 RELIGION AND THE CHURCH

Peter's religious changes were as radical as any of his other reforms. They effectively decapitated the church and made it a department of state; in fact, in a western sense he 'established' it. Some earlier Russian historians, such as Vasilii O. Klyuchevsky and P. N. Miliukov [34 *p. 45*], sought to minimise the effect of his changes. Even those who regard his reign as a watershed differ as to its effect. To Kartashev [34 *pp. 45–9*] Peter's drastic reforms were positive, enabling the church to raise its cultural standards and to widen and invigorate its missionary activities, but to Zernov they were mostly negative, since they turned bishops and clergy into mere functionaries of the state [34 *pp. 50–6*]. Peter reformed the church partly because he feared it, partly because he saw it as a hindrance to the influx of Western culture, and partly because he saw it as a source of wealth. Once in his control it could also act as a department of state, as a means both of political control and social welfare and education.

THE RUSSIAN CHURCH BEFORE PETER

Under Peter's two pious predecessors, Michael (1613–45) and Alexis (1645–76), court life was quasi-monastic. Always deeply spiritual, Russian Orthodoxy in the late seventeenth century had become obsessed with petty dogmatism, though Filaret – Michael Romanov's father and patriarch from 1619 – was as much a statesman as a cleric, 'a Wolsey magnified to the Russian scale' [31 *p. 105*]. Alexis's patriarch, Nikon, was also a supporter of reform, but tackled it by ruthlessly replacing Russian Orthodox forms with Greek. The resentment thus caused created schism and the consequent rise of the Old Believers (*starovertsi*),* known to opponents as *raskolniki** or schismatics. Nikon fell out with Alexis, was tried by a church court and banished (1666), but the church as a whole accepted his reforms, even though the *starovertsi* survived as a potent force. Nikon's two successors in Peter's reign, Joachim and Adrian, were by contrast dogmatically conservative.

Pre-Petrine Muscovy had been a free association of two independent bodies, church and state, with a delicate balance struck between patriarch and tsar. The tsar, a father figure, was never more than the patriarch's equal. Although he was responsible for maintaining good order in the church, he was in no sense the church's ruler. However, by introducing western concepts Peter distorted the traditional harmony between Muscovite Church and state. He wanted the church to be little more than a department of state, helping in the development of Russian secular power. Though sensitive to the deeply-engrained spiritual aspirations of the Russian people, he was determined to sweep away or at least neuter anything that obstructed his authority.

PETER AND RELIGION

As a child of his time, Peter was basically a religious man, though in one writer's words, 'in a limited way', which another described as 'Protestant indifferentism' [38 *p. 106*; 48 *p. 138*]. Certainly no atheist, he was brought up with a respectable knowledge of the scriptures which later impressed Bishop Burnet of Salisbury (see page 14 and *Doc. 7*) and the Sorbonne fathers; biblical quotations were often on his lips. He had also developed the habit of formal worship; as tsar, he used to read the Epistle at the Liturgy* and enjoyed singing in the choir. Religious belief was at the root of the deep sense of duty he felt to his people. He was also alert to the tsar's intrinsically spiritual role as agent of God's will and protector of Orthodoxy. Nevertheless, Peter lacked the spiritual devotion so typical of the Russian. He neither appreciated the beauty of the Russian liturgy, nor had he the intellectual interest in theological niceties that, for instance, characterised Henry VIII. Yet he had met western Erastianism* firsthand in the Lutheran and Anglican traditions, where the Church was subordinate to the secular power. His extensive talks in England with Bishop Burnet of Salisbury (1698) and with Gallican-minded fathers at the Sorbonne (1717) impressed upon him the value of the Crown-Church relationship. Indeed, he was much closer to the growing religious rationalism and secular 'territorialism' of the West [34 *p. 47*] than to Muscovite Orthodoxy, for even in Catholic states ultramontane papalism* was held at arm's length. Even Peter's lavish expenditure on the beautiful new Alexander Nevskii monastery in St Petersburg can be viewed as enhancing the authority of the secular power. Nevskii was no saint, but, like Peter, a secular warrior who had been victorious over the Swedes. He was thus, in a sense, a forerunner of Peter himself.

As his empire expanded, Peter had to consider the wide range of faiths it contained – Lutherans in the newly acquired Baltic provinces, Catholics, Uniates and Jews in the Ukraine, Muslims in the south and animists in Siberia. His Western travels, his innate rationalism and his foreign friends influenced him towards toleration. His circle included Franz Lefort, a nominal Calvinist, and Patrick Gordon, a devout Scottish Catholic. Peter was interested enough in Luther to make jottings about him in his personal notebook in 1711. Between 1699 and 1705 he allowed both Czech Jesuits and Lutherans from Germany to run schools in Moscow. In 1702 he issued a decree declaring general religious toleration of all non-Orthodox Christian faiths. But this was implemented only where pragmatism demanded it. In the new Baltic provinces, for example, Lutheranism was permitted, as were mixed marriages between Orthodox and Lutherans or Catholics from 1721 onwards [17 *pp. 171–2*]. Likewise for practical reasons Peter was tolerant of Old Believers at Olonets and at Vyg, provided they were good ironworkers. But his claim, expressed in 1709, to be tolerant to Muslims and pagans, *inozemtsy*, was false. He was hostile to Jews, and when it came to Orthodox missionary zeal he was little different from his predecessors, unless some practical reason persuaded him to adopt a different course. He forced conversion on the Tatars in Kazan in 1714, and he sent priests to China, despite his fears of a clash with Austrian Jesuits in Peking. Even so, a newly consecrated bishop, Innokentii, was ordered to conceal his episcopal orders in Peking. In common with other eighteenth-century European rulers, Peter regarded the Jesuits as a political threat and in 1719 he expelled them [*Doc. 30*], much earlier than in many west European states, such as Portugal (1759), France (1764), and Spain (1767).

Peter's distaste for traditional Orthodoxy is best exemplified by the 'Most Drunken Synod',* founded in 1692 as a black parody of the church [*Doc. 27*]. Participating in its outrageous ceremonies, his cronies were mock-patriarch and mock-priests, he himself a mere deacon. The 'patriarch' was Matvei Filimonovich, a drunkard relative, succeeded eventually by Nikita M. Zotov (1701–18). Hard though it is to understand Peter's motivation, it does coincide with his quirky psychological make-up and his penchant for practical jokes. Absurd and puerile though the 'Synod' seems to us, it was clearly important to Peter, for he not only wrote and revised the complex regulations himself, but was still attending meetings in the last weeks of his life, despite sickness. Its more serious purpose may have been to discredit Muscovite religion and thus make reform essential, but it also reflected the psychological imbalance, the darker side of Peter's nature.

THE AGENTS OF CHANGE

Certainly the church was not without fault. The quality of the clergy was poor, their intellectual and moral standard exceptionally low. The married secular priests were almost a hereditary caste and monastic vocation had become a convenient form of draft-dodging. Peter saw the danger of the superabundance of monks and nuns, 14,000 and 10,000 respectively (more than twice as many as in the English monasteries at their dissolution in the 1530s) and believed the proliferation of abbeys in Constantinople had contributed to its fall to the Turks in 1453. Clerical wealth was all-pervasive; there were 557 monasteries and convents which owned 130,000 peasant households; of these, 20,000 were in the hands of one house, the Troitsa-Sergeev. The patriarch had 9,000 peasant households and the Metropolitan* of Rostov 4,400. Like Henry VIII, Peter saw the monasteries as a ripe plum for a ruler desperate for revenue. The 1722 Supplement to the *Dukhovnyi Reglament** [57 p. 252] therefore decreed that in future no one under 50 years of age could take monastic vows. He would have liked to go further and turn all existing monasteries and convents into hospitals and schools.

Three clerics from Kiev, remarkably similar in background, were the driving force behind Peter's reforms. Stefan Yavorskii and Feofan Prokopovich were Ukrainian, Theodosius Yanovskii was of polonised south-west Russian noble stock. More cultured and outward-looking than Russia, the Ukraine had already been a potent influence on the Russian church since the mid-seventeenth century. Indeed the Kiev school, which was given the status of Academy in 1701, was one of scores founded in eastern Europe as part of the Counter-Reformation.

Stefan Yavorskii (1658–1722), trained partly under the Jesuits in Lvov and subsequently to be professor of philosophy at the prestigious Kiev Academy, was theoretically Peter's senior prelate from 1700 to 1722. Instead of replacing Adrian as Patriarch, Peter made Yavorskii Metropolitan of Ryazan in Russia in April 1700. Branded as a 'Latiniser'* and a foreigner by conservatives, his reforming zeal and Ukrainian-trained intellect were at first much to Peter's liking and they worked well together, but from 1710 their relationship cooled. For reasons of conscience Yavorskii refused to marry Peter's niece, Anna, to a Lutheran in 1710, and in 1714 Peter had to caution him for intemperate criticism of Protestants in a book which showed his Jesuit background. He then refused to participate in the consecration of Feofan Prokopovich as Bishop of Pskov in June 1718 and led the church's recommendation for mercy for tsarvich Alexis. Little wonder he and Peter were estranged. Despite his quasi-patriarchal position and his titular presidency of the Holy Synod, Yavorskii had lost virtually all influence by 1720.

Another highly influential churchman was Feofan Prokopovich (1681–1736), Peter's chief ecclesiastical propagandist after 1718. Trained partly in a Polish Jesuit College, in Switzerland and in Rome, he returned to Kiev, where he became Rector in 1711. Peter called him to Moscow in October 1716, where he was consecrated Bishop of Pskov two years later. Honoured with the courtesy title of archbishop (1720), he became second vice-president of the Synod, which he thenceforth dominated. His Western training gave him familiarity with, and sympathy for, Western Erastianism and French Gallicanism.* Increasingly cosmopolitan and Protestant in taste and theology as the years passed, Prokopovich was as hostile to 'Latinisers' as to traditional Russian clergy. A scholarly man with a library of 3,000 books, he had introduced mathematical and scientific studies to the Kiev Academy in 1707. He became a member of Peter's Neptune Society for the advancement of science, a body of Russians and qualified foreigners. With good reason he has been called 'the first authentic voice in Russia of the Early Enlightenment' [57 *p. 54*]. In sermons and in his *Pravda volimonarshei* (The Justice of the Monarch's Will) of 1722, he advocated monarchical absolutism. Western thinkers such as Grotius and Hobbes were his mentors. After Peter's death Prokopovich devoted the rest of his days – he died in 1736 – to championing the tsar's ideas and what later came to be called 'enlightened absolutism'.

Also significant was Theodosius Yanovskii (c. 1650–1726) who had studied at Kiev Academy between 1663 and 1673 before becoming a monk in Moscow. After a spell as senior administrator of the historic Novgorod diocese, he became 'ecclesiastical judge' for St Petersburg and the new Baltic provinces, almost a new diocese in itself, independent of other prelates and close to Peter. He officiated at the marriage of Peter's niece, Anna, to the Duke of Courland in

1710 and two years later was appointed archimandrite* of the new Nevskii monastery, so important for Petrine propaganda. Yanovskii helped to compose the new episcopal oath of 1716 and the manifesto of 25 January 1721. By 1718 he was more influential than Yavorskii. As first vice-president of the Synod in 1721 he shared with Prokopovich the role of Peter's main channel of communication with the Synod. He fell from grace after Peter's death by antagonising Menshikov. Accused of peculation, he was arrested, accused of high treason, publicly condemned and sentenced to life imprisonment in a Karelian monastery where he died in February 1726.

Patriarch Adrian's death in October 1700 gave Peter his chance to push ahead with reform of the church. Preoccupied with the disaster at Narva, he initially appointed Yavorskii as acting patriarch only as a temporary measure, but later decided to make it permanent. In his own words, Russians had come to look on the patriarch 'as a second sovereign, equal in power to the autocrat himself, or even above him' [48 *p. 145*]. However, Peter saw things differently. He wanted Yavorskii to be no more than a useful tool to preach at and plan celebrations for military victories, to advise on ecclesiastical appointments and, when necessary, to anathematise political opponents such as Mazepa. Apart from this Yavorskii merely administered the Ryazan and Moscow dioceses. Patriarchal and church finances, which were out of his hands, were administered by a revived *monastyrskii prikaz** under Peter's own control.

CONTROL OF THE CHURCH'S WEALTH

By letting patriarchal power lapse, Peter gained administrative control of the church. In particular, the revival of the *monastyrskii prikaz* gave him control over its finances. Peter's attitude in this matter must be seen against the background of his desperate need for money in time of war; in 1711 he instructed the Senate to 'collect as much money as possible, for money is the artery of war' [57 *p. 80*]. Government control over church finance was nothing new. Peter had issued decrees in 1696 and 1697 restricting clerical expenditure and directing surplus ecclesiastical revenue to the crown. Though monastic wealth was intended for social and educational purposes and to improve parish life, it was often siphoned off for military needs. This was not always the case, however. In 1706 Peter used funds provided by the *monastyrskii prikaz* to establish a surgical hospital and medical school in

Moscow, administered by the Dutch physician, Nicholaas Bidloo, and Heinrich Röpken. Between 1708 and 1712 this treated nearly 2,000 patients and until 1720 supported the training of 35 to 40 students. By then the *monastyrskii prikaz's* annual 'hospital' budget amounted to almost 5,000 roubles. A Scotsman, Robert Erskine, who was Peter's personal physician (*leibmedik*) for fourteen years, reorganised Russian medical administration as *arkhiater* (chief physician) [86 in 20 *p. 197*]. In addition, the monasteries were instructed to care for disabled soldiers, one of Peter's special concerns, and to provide almshouses. By 1721 there were 31 almshouses for males and 62 for females, with a total of 4,411 inhabitants, a tenfold increase during the course of Peter's reign.

Peter realised the need to curtail the church's expenditure. He therefore decreed that no clerics with income from land should receive a stipend, and that no new monasteries should be founded. He also abolished all clerical tax privileges and barred the priesthood to uneducated men and those under 30. In 1701 he restricted monks to an income of ten roubles per month with a fixed amount of grain or firewood. As for bishops, they were required to hand over at least 50 per cent of their income to the *monastyrskii prikaz* or to local officials. Yavorskii himself had to hand over the bulk of his revenue to the Admiralty *prikaz*, and be content with income from the vacant see of Tambov. Yet, though Peter used church wealth to finance his expensive foreign policy, as well as to encourage social welfare, he did not seize the church's lands, as had happened in many countries in western Europe. It was left to his successors to take this final step, in 1764.

THE HOLY SYNOD

If church finance helped Peter's overall aims, his second administrative onslaught was even more significant; it enabled him to use the church directly as an arm of government. The key legislation for this, proclaimed in a manifesto of 25 January 1721, was the *Dukhovnyi Reglament* (Spiritual Regulation), of which Prokopovich was the principal author. It has been hailed by historians as his 'greatest literary achievement and the most enduring monument to his genius' [57 *p. 60*]. Peter took a hand in its revision; indeed, the influence of his discussions with Burnet in England (1698) and with the Sorbonne fathers (1717) can clearly be seen. Simultaneously the *Dukhovnyi Reglament* established a spiritual *kollegiya*, later known as the Holy Synod, and laid down detailed regulations for the church and its clergy. Furthermore, it empowered the *kollegiya* to develop and extend the reforms it set out.

The new *kollegiya* was intended to be parallel to the new secular colleges. Though at first called the *dukhovnaya kollegiya* (Spiritual College) it was technically superior to them and of equal importance to the Senate. However, to appease conservative sentiments Peter soon renamed it *svyateisheii pravitel' stvuyushchii sinod* (the Most Holy Directing Synod). Though the word *sinod* was new to Russian language, *svyateisheii* (Most Holy) was of special significance, since it had formerly been reserved for the Patriarch alone. Moreover, *pravitel' stvuyushchii* (All-Ruling) had earlier been an attribute solely of the Senate. It was clearly Peter's intention, then, that the Synod should take the place of both the patriarch and existing church councils. Although based on Western Erastian practice, this was a new phenomenon for Orthodoxy. Like the secular *kollegiya* the Synod had a president, Yavorskii, two vice-presidents, Yanovskii and Prokopovich, and eight other members, all drawn from the clergy. The tsar nominated every one of the members, the church none, and all had to take an additional oath that the tsar was 'Final Judge of this College' [*Doc. 28*]. The *Monastyrskii Prikaz* was thus replaced, only to reappear later as a subordinate organ of the Synod.

Though the Synod was given spiritual status and was even substituted for the Patriarch amongst the prayers in the Litany, it was, unlike him, the tsar's instrument. All bishops, except one, were required to sign the *Regulation*. Given the choice of agreeing or facing dismissal, they all agreed. Nor did Peter consult foreign Orthodox patriarchs, as tradition dictated. They too were confronted with the *fait accompli*, with little alternative but to recognise the Holy Synod as 'their holy brother in Christ' [38 p. 111] in place of the Patriarch of Moscow. They did so in 1723.

Despite its elevated position, the Synod was no patriarch, nor had it the strength of the Senate. Its first title, Spiritual College, was more appropriate, for it was Peter's tool. Peter's distrust of the clergy was clear. Though Yanovskii was the obvious choice as Yavorskii's successor in 1722, Peter, in fact, replaced Yavorskii with a new official, the *Oberprokuror* (Chief Procurator), who was to be *stryapchii*, 'our eye and personal representative' [57 p. 176]. The *Prokuror* was usually an army officer. The first was I. V. Boltin, a colonel of the Dragoons, who attended regularly, resplendent in military uniform. His duty was to report any disobedience in the Synod directly to Peter himself, but unlike his late nineteenth-century successors, Boltin earned the Synod's gratitude for not interfering much, and retired soon after Peter's death.

The Synod itself was unrepresentative of the Russian church as a whole, for in June 1724 its eleven members consisted of five Ukrainians, three Great Russians, two Greeks and one Serb. This, however, was excusable, for skilled leadership was essential in a period of rapid reform, and the Synod was an enlightened group of academics and monks. Prokopovich and Yavorskii at least were churchmen of European stature.

PETER'S AUTHORITY OVER THE CHURCH

Peter demonstrated his authority over the church in other ways. It was Peter as tsar, not the patriarch, who ordered the anathematisation of Mazepa, 'the second Judas'. It was Peter as tsar who ordered all bishops to take a new oath in 1716. Though Peter never called himself Head of the Church, certainly his use of it as a department of state grew significantly and the clergy increasingly assumed the role of a secular civil service. Thus the church was bound to the new tsarist bureaucracy, more so than in western states, both Catholic and Protestant, though there were remarkable similarities to Anglican Erastianism. It was henceforth the clergy who were to announce new taxes to their congregations, a common enough arrangement throughout Europe. By the *Spiritual Regulation* priests were also to administer oaths of tsarist loyalty to all except peasants. As in England post-1538, they were to keep a record of births, marriages and deaths in registers, *metriki*, and send in analyses to their bishops for the use of the Synod. Though this instruction was never fully implemented, the intention was clear; the clergy were to be registrars for the state.

Furthermore, priests were to be used for political control, offensive though it might have been to tender consciences [*Doc. 29*]. They were to reveal information given under seal of the confessional, if there was criminal intention, especially in the case of 'evil ideas and impenitent intent against the Sovereign' [59 *p. 61*]. They were also to 'root out thieves, rebels, bandits, fugitive soldiers and similar people' [57 *p. 99*].

Much more sinister was Peter's use of the church as promoter and guardian of loyalty. One can detect here the growth of an eighteenth-century personality cult. Prayers were to be said for the tsar and family, using the new titles of 'Emperor' and 'Empress' and Peter's new epithet 'the Great'. As part of this glorification of the ruler, the body of Alexander Nevskii, a thirteenth-century warrior who in effect was adopted as patron saint of the Petrine Empire, was interred on 30 August 1724 with full honours in St Petersburg's new Nevskii monastery – a fitting shrine for the revitalised monarchy. In addition, Prokopovich's *Primer*, first published in March 1720, enjoined filial obedience to the ecclesiastical and civil authorities by quoting the fifth commandment, 'Honour thy father'. Its chief purpose was to instil respect for the paternalistic authority of the tsar. Press censorship was delegated to the Synod, acting in the tsar's name.

By 1725 the church was an arm of the tsar's government as never before, and was to remain so until 1917. Despite Russia's powerful spiritual tradition the church was too weak to defend itself. Enfeebled by Alexis's victory over patriarch Nikon, by divisions between 'Old Believers' and the mainstream church, as well as between secular and monastic clergy, and between a wealthy hierarchy and the parish clergy, it was powerless. In his endeavour to root out corruption, slackness and disloyalty Peter was supported by a phalanx of able, intellectual clerics, especially from the Ukraine, but there was no strong protagonist to defend the church's own authority. The reign saw the victory of Prokopovich's Erastian Protestant influence over Yavorskii's more Catholicising approach. What the church gained in political power and privilege it lost spiritually in its role as shepherd of the Russian people.

R.T.C. LIBRARY, LETTERKENNY

9 OPPOSITION TO PETER

THE CAUSES OF OPPOSITION

Muscovy had always been xenophobic, conservative in ethos, and resistant to change. Opposition therefore was not new, but under Peter it became 'constant and pervasive', as it had never been before. In fact, as one writer has put it, 'The history of opposition to Peter is in effect the history of his reign' [20 p. 258-9]. Opposition was inevitable from the high officials displaced in the palace revolution of 1689; from the peasantry, groaning under the continuing burdens of serfdom; and from the Old Believers, the *raskolniki*, who were already hostile before Peter's accession. But Peter exacerbated all this by his policies and his personal behaviour. The unprecedentedly high taxation to pay for war, the enforced cultural changes in dress, tobacco smoking and beard shaving, calendar reform and restriction on church privileges, his use of western, not Russian, architects for St Petersburg – all these made matters worse. But recent scholarship [20 p. 270; 38 p. 140] shows that it was Peter's personal behaviour which caused the deepest offence. His heavy drinking and smoking, his western (usually shabby) dress, his daily manual labour both in carpentry and metalwork, were all regarded as unbefitting for a tsar. Add to this the abandonment of his highborn Muscovite first wife for a foreign peasant girl, his brutality towards his son, Alexis, his Holy Drunken Synod, his friendships with foreigners and his prolonged visits abroad, his evident dislike for Holy Moscow, his love of the sea and ships, so alien to Muscovites, and there is a recipe for widespread personal antipathy, even hostility. The tsar, no longer a sacrosanct figure above criticism, was exposed as a man of folly. He was castigated by his critics as a 'tyrant', 'impostor', 'Anti-Christ', 'heretic', 'blasphemer', 'Latiniser', 'iconoclast', 'really a "German" or a "Swede" from Stekolny town,' (i.e. Stockholm), even a 'Musulman in disguise' [20 p. 270; 34 p. 68].

We can separate out the opposition to Peter into three categories:

first, the *streltsy* at the beginning of the reign; second the *boyars* and peasants; and third sections of the church. The 50,000 *streltsy*, as supporters of Peter's dynastic rivals, the Miloslavkys, were a potent force, especially after Alexis's sudden death in 1676, when, as we have seen, they supported Feodor (1676–82). In the brief struggle following Feodor's demise in 1682 they supported Sophia and the Miloslavsky faction against Peter. In May 1682, as we have noted, they brutally cut down the progressive Matveev at the Kremlin before Peter's eyes. Again in August 1689 the *streltsy* were Sophia's instrument in her abortive coup to remove Peter at Preobrazhenskoe. The fact that the last of these episodes ended with Peter and his Naryshkin relatives in the saddle may have temporarily silenced them, but it did nothing to endear the *streltsy* to Peter.

THE *STRELTSY*

The *streltsy's* successful bids for power in 1676 and 1682, the failed attempt in 1689 and an abortive plot in February 1697 led by Ivan Zickler, were menacing enough, but all these pale into insignificance before the serious *streltsy* revolt of 1698, when Peter was absent in the West. So threatening was it that he cut short his visit to Vienna and dashed back home. Besides the conservatives' grievances, already mentioned, the *streltsy* especially resented the mid-century rise to importance of the 'new formation'* regiments. This was intensified by the fact that the *streltsy* had recently been posted far away from Moscow and had been given the most dangerous part in the defence of Azov, resulting in many casualties. Mercifully for Peter, the disorganised *streltsy* march on Moscow, which began in June 1698, was easily put down by Shein and Gordon 40 kilometres west of the city. The result was that 130 of the rebels were hanged and 2,000 exiled.

Nevertheless, Peter felt alarmed enough on his return to begin his own investigations. Interrogations under torture as well as executions began in September 1698. Twelve *boyars* under Prince Feodor Romodanovsky, head of the *Preobrazhenskii prikaz* and governor of Moscow, investigated twenty suspects each day. Peter himself probably took part in the interrogation, but modern scholarship no longer supports the contemporary view that he personally took a hand in the actual torture and executions [38]. In three weeks in October 1698 just under 800 *streltsy* met their death, and a further 350 were killed in February 1699. Compared with the terrors perpetrated under Ivan IV and Stalin this was 'an operation of almost surgical precision' [78 *p. 12*]. Though probably not implicated herself, Peter's half-sister, Sophia, was even more closely confined in her convent in full view of the Kremlin walls where the *streltsy* corpses were exposed, three of them directly opposite her cell. As Keep has shown, Peter's claim in his journal that he summarily disbanded the *streltsy* is not supported by recent scholarship, for as late as 1705–1706 between 60 and 70 per cent of the rebels at Astrakhan were *streltsy*. They were also recorded as being present at Kiev and Viborg in 1710–11 [67].

THE *BOYARS* AND PEASANTS

Though the *streltsy* ceased to be a major threat after 1698, the *boyars* and the peasants were a potential source of trouble. For the *boyars*, increased permanent state service was irksome. Compulsory and lifelong from the age of fifteen, it meant prolonged absence from their families and, even more significant perhaps, their estates; it could even entail compulsory naval training abroad.

Among the leading dissenting *boyars* was Avram Lopukhin, Peter's own brother-in-law, who was eventually executed in 1718. There were also the Sokovnin and the Pushkin families, who were involved in the Zickler conspiracy of 1697. Nevertheless, the *boyars* as a class had already been conditioned to some state service for many years, and when it came to the point, they offered little opposition. Indeed, some of Peter's reforms improved their lot; for instance, there was an increase in the number of posts available to them in the navy or diplomatic service. Some *boyars*, endowed with foresight if not with altruism, recognised the intrinsic value of the tsar's reforms for future Russian development and learnt to adapt. For others the mystique surrounding the tsar remained a potent factor, as we can see from their writings. There were also *boyars* who, like the self-made men of wealth, gave positive, forthright support to the new policies. The comment of a reformer, Ivan Pososhkov, himself an industrialist and merchant of peasant stock, is well-known; the Tsar, he wrote, 'pulls uphill with less than a dozen helpers, while millions pull downhill' [34 *p. 68*]. But this was only true as far as the masses were concerned, for the seeds of reform were already present in the minds of the best men among the nobility even before Peter. There was substantial support in the ranks of upper middle-class men too whose views owed nothing to Peter's immediate influence. Feodor Saltykov, who had been naval representative of the Russian government in London, provides a notable example. By independently arguing – in his *Declaration* and *Propositions* of 1713–14 – for a large-scale adoption of aspects of life he had found in England he anticipated many reforms Peter was about to launch. There was also widespread support from those who had been influenced by the inflow of western ideas, most notably from Poland and the Ukraine, throughout the seventeenth century. Many of this group had seen the need for dramatic transformation as early as the aftermath of the Time of Troubles.

The peasants resented being hauled out of their village life, harsh though it already was, to serve in the armed services or to die as labourers in the swamps, building St Petersburg, digging canals or engaged on other major projects. Life for them was more brutal than ever. Fed with hostile propaganda from the church and the conservative *boyars*, they looked upon Peter with the revulsion we have already noted.

THE CHURCH

Despite significant elements among the *boyars* which supported Peter, they remained as a group a potential danger for much of the reign. But the most intractable group was the church, or rather large portions of it. The church was by far the most conservative section of society. Despite, and perhaps because of, Peter's refusal to appoint a successor to Patriarch Adrian (1700), it remained a potent focus of opposition. Little wonder that Peter sought control over it, at first through Yavorskii, then through the Synod, and, finally, through Prokopovich, the Ukrainian Archbishop of Novgorod.

Opposition was nowhere stronger than among the group of Old Believers, *starovertsi* or *raskolniki*, who had vigorously opposed Patriarch Nikon's significant mid-century reforms especially in the Liturgy, finally made official in 1667. Nowhere was religious conservatism more rigid and unyielding than in seventeenth-century Russia. Reactions to Nikon's reforms had been strong and violent. Fed by the writings of conservatives such as Grigorii Talitskii, the book copyist and popular religious teacher (*nachetchik*) who was tried and executed in 1700–1, the Old Believers declared the church under Nikon to have been apostate. Holy Muscovy, the Third Rome, had already fallen from grace. Now, under Peter the Anti-Christ, Moscow had become another Babylon.

The end of the world was at hand. The political implications of the Old Believers' attitude were inflammatory. If the church was in apostasy and Russia in the grip of Anti-Christ, then obedience to the tsar was sinful, even blasphemous. Here was a recipe for revolt, not just opposition; subjects were positively encouraged to civil disobedience and refusal to pay taxes. Talitskii, indeed, had apparently planned to denounce and replace Peter while he was away campaigning in the late 1690s. Seventeen persons named as collaborators by Talitskii under torture were committed for trial; five were executed, eight flogged, mutilated and exiled to Siberia. The Talitskii case, often referred to by Peter in later years, even as late as 1708 and twice in 1722, became for him the 'touchstone of his obsession', fear of revolt [20 *p. 268–9*]. James Cracraft suggests that one of Peter's recorded dreams is relevant; in it an eagle (representing Peter himself) savages a 'large, wild beast, like a crocodile or a dragon' (the opposition). This may relate not only to his own inner struggle between his acts of vilest cruelty and those of heroic kingship, but also – confusedly, as is common in dreams – to his obsession with the *raskolniki* who often depicted him, in word and picture, as the '*krokodil*' [20 *p. 243–6*].

A notable section of the church, however, supported the tsar. Indeed, on Peter's orders Yavorskii wrote *The Signs of the Coming of the Anti-Christ and the End of Time*, a counterblast to the conservatives. The Time of Troubles had made many Russians realise that some form of transformation or rejuvenation was essential, but though an increasingly vociferous and influential minority looked to the West, the majority still wanted renewal from the old Russian roots, from the old Orthodox tradition. However, in a quarter of a century of frenetic energy Peter's dynamic changes swept along all, even conservatives, often against their will. To extreme traditionalists Peter's answers were wrong; Holy Russia's duty was to shun not only infidels in the East and foreigners in the West, but even the so-called 'Greek' reform of Nikon. For them Peter's call for Westernisation had a religious connotation. Seen in this light, Peter's insistence on Western dress and beard shaving was a tactical blunder, for these reforms focused on the vital external symbols that marked out Holy Russia. The Fathers of the Church had used Old Testament sources to support the kaftan and the beard; indeed a shaven man was denied a funeral mass. Whether the Orthodox fathers were theologically correct or not, these traditions were engrained in Russian lives. Some shaven men even carried their beards under their coats in case of sudden death, so they could be buried by Orthodox rites. Symbols are more potent than theories, and Peter's enforcement of symbolic change was as dangerous as any of his practical policies.

Even in the more conservative Sophia's reign these *raskolniki* had drawn into their circle other oppressed and disaffected groups, such as the serfs and the Cossacks. Persecution of the *raskolniki* had been a central part of Sophia's policy, and in December 1684 she had issued a decree ordering that they should be searched out and tortured. Burning at the stake, by the late seventeenth century outmoded in the West, was used for those who refused to recant. Some Old Believers, like mediaeval Cathars, only avoided falling into the hands of Anti-Christ by self-incineration.

Because of his own rationalist views and the political necessity to turn a blind eye, Peter was more liberal than Sophia. He saw it as vital to encourage the immigration of foreign technical experts, whatever their faith, and to allow them to settle unmolested. If he was to prosecute the prolonged struggle with Sweden successfully, persecution of his fellow-countrymen was a luxury he and Russia could not afford. Accordingly, as we have seen (page 56), in 1703 he allowed the *raskolniki* group centred on Vyg in Karelia to worship in peace, as long as they produced sufficient quantities of iron ore. Later, in 1709, he allowed another group of *raskolniki* to return from the Baltic provinces where they had fled years before. In 1715 *raskolniki* in the Ukraine were rewarded with grants of land and freedom of worship because of their role as guerrillas in opposing Charles XII's invasion. Pragmatism, as usual, was the touchstone of Peter's policy.

REPRESSION

Though Peter became so obsessed with the pervasiveness of opposition to his regime, we need to keep the scale of repression in perspective. The total executed after the *streltsy* and Astrakhan revolts was not above 1,000. This was no Stalinist purge, not even a new terror on the model of Ivan IV. There was no repetition of Ivan's notorious *Oprichnina* (1565) with its band of 6,000 horsemen in black, carrying emblems of a dog's head and broom to signify the sniffing out and sweeping away of treason, followed by wholesale orgies of brutality. Peter's retribution was rational and narrowly focused on actual offenders. But because, throughout his reign, he adopted a policy of harsh repression towards opponents, there was little overt revolt. Only on four occasions was he faced with open opposition – namely, the *Streltsy* uprising in 1698, the Astrakhan mutiny in 1705–6, Bulavin's Cossack rebellion in 1707 and the peasant revolt in the Volga basin in 1709–10.

Peter's main tool for political control was the *Preobrazhenskii prikaz*, the former administrative heart of the *Preobrazhenskii* and *Semenovskii* regiments. Originally there to safeguard public order in Moscow in place of the discredited *streltsy*, it had been given increased responsibility to investigate political offences. Still acting under the Mayor of Moscow, Prince Feodor Romodanovski, it interrogated and punished Russians of all ranks, ranging from nobles who had tried to evade state service to insignificant drunks accused of making jokes about the tsar. It continued to deal with political offences even after the foundation of the *Yustitz kollegiya* in 1719, and could claim to be the first truly centralised organ of government.

What constituted a political offence was decided by Peter himself, though the code of 1649 had included attempts against the tsar's life and plots against the government. A senate decree of 1714 defined political offences more specifically. Conspiracy to kill the tsar or to rebel was an obvious case, but so was any joint action, even group petitioning, that could be interpreted as undermining the tsar's authority. Between 1697 and 1708 the *prikaz* heard hundreds of cases, involving plots, rebellion, espionage and 'unseemly utterances'. Excluding the *streltsy* revolt, there were convictions in 507 cases (1697–1708). 'Unseemly utterances' was the commonest political offence between 1697 and 1708 [20 *p. 262–3*]. The *ustav voinskii* of 1716 widened the scope of political crime to include the mere imagining or wish to carry out a disloyal action.

All subjects, even serfs, were under obligation to denounce those suspected of plotting or careless talk by the invocation of the 'Word and Deed' procedure. Failure to do so meant death. By this means a local official could present suspects to the Preobrazhenskii Office, where interrogation was carried out with the aid of torture, usually by the knout. After sentence, the punishment was carried out – in the case of death, either by quartering, breaking on the wheel, beheading or hanging. Lesser punishments included knouting, slitting of the tongue, ripping of nostrils, or indelible branding with the words *KAT* (convict) or *VOR* (criminal) on forehead and cheek. In the case of females, compulsory spinning for the state was the preferred alternative.

Methods used in the *Preobrazhenskii prikaz* were transferred to other areas, for instance in military discipline through the Military Statute (*ustav voinskii*) of 1716, and in the attack on religious nonconformity in 1718. However, the records of the *Preobrazhenskii prikaz* reveal that all social ranks were involved in political opposition. 'Qualitatively, if not quantitatively, it would seem, Peter I faced by 1708 a kind of national resistance' [20 *p. 263*).

THE TSARVICH ALEXIS

The focus for opposition was Tsarvich Alexis. Born in February 1690, he was the only surviving son of Peter's first marriage to Evdokia Lopukhina. Peter was proud of him at birth, but after he broke with Evdokia in 1698 Peter entrusted Alexis to the care of his sister Natalia in Preobrazhenskoe. This traumatic removal, together with his own genetic make-up and the treatment of his guardians combined to make the tsarvich introverted, lacking in self-confidence, and later turned him into a heavy drinker. In any case he and his father were totally different both in character and interests. Peter was vigorous, energetic and practical, Alexis physically and intellectually lazy, despite his interest in books. Even when intellectually stirred, he was drawn to theology and the church, preferring the company of priests to scientists, technologists and mariners. It was Moscow, with its cathedrals and churches, its history and legend, that he loved.

After an abortive plan in 1698 to send him to a German court for training, Peter employed two successive German tutors, Martin Neugebauer of Danzig and Heinrich von Huyssen, to educate Alexis on German lines through the study of mathematics, languages, military exercises and dancing. Though bookish by nature, Alexis lacked the necessary intellectual vigour and deeply resented his father's attempts to dragoon him. Much worse was the brutal treatment he received at the hands of Menshikov who was charged with oversight of the tsarvich's household. Menshikov, no academic himself, coarse and often away at the battlefield, deliberately brutalised him, which only served to reinforce Alexis's introversion, lack of confidence and fear of both his father and his mentor.

Delighted as Peter was to have an heir, he was keen to make him a worthy successor by providing tasks designed to train him in statecraft. He took him on campaigns from an early age – to Archangel in 1702 and to the successful siege of Narva in 1704. He also gave him administrative work in Smolensk and Moscow three years later, but Alexis never shone and Peter grew increasingly exasperated. In Dresden, the capital of Saxony, where Peter had sent him for further military training, Alexis spent his time on mediaeval history and making extracts from the *Annales Ecclesiastici* of

Baronius. In October 1711 Peter had Alexis married to a Protestant princess, Charlotte of Brunswick-Wolfenbüttel, connected with the House of Hanover and a sister-in-law of the Habsburg Emperor. Though the marriage was dynastically suitable, in personal terms it was a failure. Alexis turned for solace to a Finnish serf-girl, Afrosina, who became his mistress.

Peter's attempt to involve Alexis in supervising ship construction at Lake Ladoga in 1713 was unsuccessful. More ominously for the tsar, Alexis was becoming the focus of opposition, for his abhorrence of the new technology and of foreign innovations attracted the conservatives, especially the 'long-beards', the conservative clergy and prominent nobles, such as Alexander Kikin and his uncle, Avram Lopukhin. The threat was real, but Peter hesitated to remove Alexis from the succession. In October 1715 he wrote a long letter to the tsarvich complaining of his lack of interest and activity: 'Better a stranger who is able than someone of one's own blood who is useless' [38 *p. 148*], he commented bitterly. In the correspondence that followed, Peter requested Alexis to change his ways or renounce the throne and enter a monastery. In October 1715 Alexis's wife, Charlotte, gave birth to a son, Peter, who survived to become the future Peter II; Charlotte herself, however, died shortly afterwards. Three weeks later Alexis's step-mother, the empress Catherine, gave birth to a son and possible heir, Peter Petrovich. Amid the general rejoicing Alexis at once offered to take monastic vows and recognise this new half-brother as heir, but tsar Peter, again taken aback, vacillated and told him to wait six months. In any case, the succession again became uncertain following Peter Petrovich's death three-and-a-half years later.

The situation was no better by the following August, when the exasperated Peter instructed Alexis to join him in Copenhagen for the forthcoming Swedish campaign. Alexis left Russia, apparently to join his father, but instead took refuge in Austria where the Emperor Charles VI hid him first in the Tyrol, then in Naples. Relations between the two countries, already cold, now became frosty. Peter, at this time in Amsterdam, feared a coup engineered by the Emperor, and Moscow was rife with rumour. Peter therefore sent the veteran diplomat, Peter Tolstoi, to Naples to negotiate Alexis's return. Ten days of discussion and a written promise of safe conduct persuaded the tsarvich to go back to Moscow in February 1718 [*Doc. 31*]. Once there, he admitted his guilt in taking flight and seeking protection from the Emperor; he then solemnly renounced his claim to the throne in favour of Peter Petrovich.

However, Peter, who was paranoid as ever, still felt threatened. Even as a monk, Alexis could be a centre of conspiracy; as one of his associates, Alexander Kikin, noted, the cowl could easily be cast aside. Fear ruled Moscow and St Petersburg in the following six months, as Peter's fear deepened and Alexis's popularity grew. From Peter's point of view, the church seemed to show Alexis unhealthy sympathy. A tide of arrests followed, and Peter, fearing the worst, ordered the *Preobrazhenskii prikaz* in Moscow and the new Secret Chancellery* (*tainaya kantselyariya*) in St Petersburg, headed by Tolstoi, to investigate Alexis's case. They uncovered proof of widespread disaffection and hostility to Peter's favourite projects, including the construction of St Petersburg, but there was no evidence of an organised plot. In the end it was Alexis's mistress, Afrosina, on whom he doted, who supplied false, but incriminating, evidence of a supposed plot between the Emperor Charles VI and Alexis to overthrow Peter. Such a plot was totally out of character for Alexis; his German mother-in-law commented: 'He prefers a rosary to a pistol' [48 *p. 107*]. Modern scholarship confirms that no such plot in fact existed, but under torture the tsarvich confessed [48 *p. 107*; 38 *p. 155*].

On 30 June and again on 5 July he was knouted, with 25 and 15 strokes respectively. Despite pleas for mercy from fourteen prominent churchmen, led by Yavorskii, a special assembly of 128 notables signed the death penalty on 3 July [*Doc. 32*] and four days later Alexis mysteriously died in the St Peter and St Paul fortress at St Petersburg, officially of apoplexy. The mystery remains, but Peter, directly or indirectly, must bear the blame. There was no mourning; in fact, on the following day, 8 July, the ninth anniversary of Poltava was celebrated with normal rejoicing and further celebrations followed on the 10th – St Peter's day in the Russian calendar. During 1718 Kikin and Dositheus, Metropolitan of Rostov, were broken on the wheel, and Avram Lophukin and four others were executed. Otherwise few suffered, compared with the terrifying aftermath of the *streltsy* revolt of 1698. Yet, though both the church and the nobility had been cowed into submission, discontent remained widespread, particularly since in Peter's last years tax burdens increased. The costly Persian campaign was a failure and there was trouble with the Turks and in the Caucasus. The trial of Alexis and the manner of his death only accentuated this discontent, but Peter's grip remained firm.

Alexis's interrogation and death had other effects. Undoubtedly the church's sympathy for him hastened the official abolition of the patriarchate. The Secret Chancellery, specifically created for the trial, remained in being: though officially abolished in 1726, it lasted in one shape or another until the nineteenth century. Between 1718 and 1725 the Secret Chancellery dealt with 370 'grave cases'. Of these over 75 per cent were for political offences, and the great majority were lodged by Peter himself – a significant demonstration of his obsession with treachery. Peter felt isolated. Gloom and anxiety reigned. Most of his old associates were dead; others seemed hostile. In December 1723 a Saxon minister wrote that Peter 'cannot find a single loyal subject apart from two foreigners who hold the reins of empire; that is Yaguzhinskii and Ostermann' [38 *p. 155*], a Lithuanian and a German. Nevertheless, Peter was unassailable. 'Just as Poltava made clear the irruption of Russian power into a largely hostile Europe, so the death of Alexis illustrated Peter's iron grip upon his own recalcitrant country' [38 *p. 154*].

As James Cracraft has noted, 'the records of both the *Preobrazhenskii prikaz* and the Secret Chancellery suggest that the problem of Peter I's opposition is also the problem of Peter himself: of his motives, ambitions and desires, if not of his whole psychological make-up' [20 *p. 265*]. Peter may have provoked opposition by the radical nature of his reforms, but he had the means and the will to crush any opponents who endangered his position, whether he had to terrorise them through his security offices, the *Preobrazhenskii prikaz* and the Secret Chancellery, or kill them as he had done his son. As he replied to a diplomat at the time, 'If a fire meets with straw and other light stuff, it soon spreads, but if it finds iron or stone in its way it is extinguished of itself' [45 *p. 698*].

10 ST PETERSBURG

THE BEGINNINGS

The construction of St Petersburg, built to order by one man, was at once the epitome of Peter's policy of Westernisation and of his own energy and enthusiasm. In Russian history there had been several changes of capital – from Novgorod to Kiev to Moscow – but the migration to St Petersburg was unique. Peter abandoned a well-populated defensible city with administrative buildings for a frequently flooded, swampy waste, recently controlled by a formidable enemy and always vulnerable. When he arrived at the site with his troops in 1703, there were, apart from two Swedish fortresses, only a few Finnish fishermen's huts. The soil was poor, the vegetation scanty. Winters were long and dark and the Neva, often frozen, was only navigable on average 218 days a year [*Doc. 37*]. In international law this part of Ingria was recognised as Swedish territory; the tsars had renounced sovereignty over it in perpetuity by the Treaty of Stobolva in 1617. But worse than that, to launch a campaign and simultaneously to build a grand new capital city so soon after Peter's humiliating defeat at Narva (1700) was daring, even foolhardy.

Soon after the capture of the Swedish fortress of Nyenskans in May 1703, Peter chose the nearby Lust-Eland (Janni-saari in Finnish – Hare Island) on the Neva delta as the site for a new fortress, initially known, in Russianised German, as Sankt' Piterburkh or, in Greek, Petropolis. In late June 1703 the St Peter and St Paul cathedral was consecrated and in autumn 1704 work started on the fortified shipyard, to be known as the Admiralty. Feodor Golovin, the captor of Nyenskans, only wanted an arsenal, but Peter, driven by his love of the sea and his wish to leave Moscow, with its conservatism and to him, hateful, continental climate, decided to make this his new capital. It would also be a strong base for his new Baltic fleet, a useful port and well placed for him to wield diplomatic influence in Europe. St Petersburg's vulnerability to

Swedish recapture in the first years [*Doc. 36*] receded noticeably after the seizure of Viborg in 1710.

PROBLEMS OF CONSTRUCTION

The Admiralty shipyard, started in 1704, was already working in 1705. From then onwards artisans, such as carpenters, smiths and their families, were drafted and forcibly settled, but it was not until after the Swedish danger had largely passed that compulsory settlement gathered apace. A series of decrees made recruitment and forced migration a continuous process. Thousands of workers poured into the embryo city. In August 1710, for instance, Peter settled 5,000 craftsmen there. He ordered wooden dwellings, shops and churches to be built to house both permanent and seasonal workers. The first stone buildings, for Golovkin, Menshikov and Peter himself (the Summer Palace), were not started until 1710. Modern research estimates that in the period 1703–25 between 10 and 30,000 persons worked in St Petersburg each year, compared with a mere 3,000 on any pre-Petrine project.

Impetuous as ever, Peter changed his plans for the city in the early years. The first dwellings were on the right bank around the fortress, but serious flooding forced all new settlements to be established on the higher left bank, where the palaces now stand. Later again, he moved the centre of activity downstream to Vasilievskii Island, so it could be crisscrossed with canals as in Amsterdam [*Doc. 37*]. This provoked opposition among the workers and the nobility. Between 1710 and 1712, 365 of a further 2,200 recruits fled and over half the 1,000 carpenters drafted by decree to St Petersburg in 1713 ran away. The nobles and gentry, in particular, objected to the fog, the cold, the floods from the river Neva, the long winters, the smaller houses and more expensive life-style of the new capital [*Doc. 40*]. One of Peter's jesters described the city as 'on one side the sea, on the other sorrow, on the third moss and on the fourth a sigh' [38 *p. 120*]. The appalling climate, the unhealthy work conditions and the delays in providing food resulted in a heavy death toll. Foreigners' contemporary estimates of 100,000 were, however, exaggerated. Modern scholarship by the Soviet historian, S.P. Luppov, reveals a figure of only several thousand deaths in total from 1703 to 1725, and that after 1710 steps were taken to ease the situation with medical care [35]. Yet, despite all the setbacks the city grew apace, from only a handful of permanent residents in 1703 to 8,000 in 1710 and 40,000 in 1725.

To foster growth Peter granted his new city commercial privileges. After 1713 it had the monopoly of the export of tar, caviar, potash and some types of leather, and in 1720 it was given preferential duties over Archangel, by now already in decline. Two years later Peter prohibited all export through the White Sea except local products. By 1724 St Petersburg had eclipsed Archangel and the newly captured Baltic ports, Viborg, Reval and Riga. In that year 180 foreign ships entered St Petersburg and only 50 into Archangel. Symbolically, Peter himself piloted the first Dutch ship into St Petersburg in 1713. Foreign merchants were encouraged or even forced to settle there, and the British 'factory' had to move from Moscow to St Petersburg in 1723.

Workers may have been moved forcibly and swiftly to the new capital, but administration was transferred more gradually; there was no formal decree. Peter ordered Golovin, his chancellor, skilled in foreign affairs, to take up residence there in 1706, just before his untimely death. By then the city had the Admiralty, its subsidiary buildings, several Orthodox and Lutheran churches, an inn and a number of cafes; many of these were made from tree trunks with roofs of potter's clay. Early in 1708 Peter invited his sister, Natalia, his two half-sisters, the tsaritsas, with others to St Petersburg [1 ff.126v, 127r]. Four years later he invited 1,000 nobles to migrate with their families and build houses of plaster and wood in 'English fashion' on the left bank opposite the fortress. The 500 rich merchants, 500 shopkeepers, 2,000 housepainters, smiths and tailors, who followed were to construct dwellings behind the fortress on the right bank. To encourage support for his city, Peter invested it, as we have already seen, with a historical dimension by founding the Alexander Nevskii monastery on the supposed site of Nevskii's victory over the Swedes in 1242.

TOWN PLANNING

The city was the first in Russia to have a positive plan. Though Peter showed personal interest in the building of the fortress from 1703 onwards, it was only from 1706 that he became intensely involved in the planning of the city itself [*Doc. 36*]. Domenico Trezzini, an Italian architect who already had relevant experience of coping with Copenhagen's boggy suburbs, arrived in 1705 as chief architect of 'Urban Affairs', in charge of the overall design. Peter, already deeply influenced by the merchant houses of Amsterdam and Wren's work with London churches and at Kensington Palace, relied greatly on Trezzini. Even at the height of the war, they worked together on detailed plans for the graded houses of the nobility, the well-to-do and the poor. It was Trezzini who began the Summer Palace in 1710, the Winter Palace in 1711, and in 1712 the St Peter and St Paul Cathedral, the height of whose slender spire was to exceed that of Moscow's tallest building, Ivan the Great's belltower. He also translated into stone Peter's plan to have the administrative colleges under one roof.

Trezzini laid down general regulations for the city [*Docs. 37* and *39*]. All houses were to have their fronts abutting onto the streets, not in courtyards in traditional Russian fashion. The skyline was to be regular; even Peter's Winter Palace had to conform. In 1711 Peter had a model cottage built from which others were to be copied. After 1714 all buildings were meant to conform to Trezzini's plans [*Docs. 37* and *39*], though in fact this later proved impossible to enforce. Though for ordinary houses wood and then wattle and daub, in Prussian style, were employed in the early years, Peter made a determined effort to get stone used where possible. The visual impact would be greater and fire risks lessened. To encourage masons to move to St Petersburg and thus hasten the transition, Peter forbade stone housebuilding elsewhere (1714) [*Doc. 39*]. However, ordinary houses continued to be built of wood, and fires were still frequent in the 1720s.

In contrast with other cities St Petersburg, situated on a delta of islands astride the Neva River, was strictly divided into areas – Admiralty workers lived on Admiralty Island, skilled workers on Gorodskii Island, landowners on Vassilievski Island. With the arrival of Leblond, the French architect, in 1716, construction of the city began in earnest, with the commissioning of 700 to 1,000 large stone houses a year and 500 to 700 others. However, by 1725 only a quarter of all the houses commissioned had been built, and half were of wood. Furthermore, Leblond's ambitious plan to build the city with a regular street-plan in a neat, elliptical shape was rejected as too expensive. Peter himself at first felt more at home with the less ostentatious architectural style of Amsterdam; the climate and setting were similar, but strangely there was no Dutch architect employed at St Petersburg until the 1720s. Peter's visit to Paris in 1717 persuaded him of the need for size to impress foreigners. Hence the construction of Apraksin's magnificent three-storied palace (on the site of the present Winter Palace) and of Menshikov's on Vassilievski Island which was carried out in the imposing Italian style. The standard of planning in St Petersburg was more thorough than in most Western cities of the period, and as the years passed amenities increased. By the end of the reign nearly 600 street lamps, fired with hempseed oil, had been installed and the streets paved, including the whole Nevskii Prospekt. In June 1714 a twice weekly post to Moscow was introduced. After 1720 no cattle were allowed on the streets. For all this work, brick production on a massive scale was a prerequisite. Eleven million bricks were made in 1710 and 10 million a year after that, but by 1720 even these vast amounts were not enough and bricks had to be imported. Glass was rare; mica was used even for nobles' houses, while the poor had recourse to animal bladders. An estimated 80 per cent of the workforce in 1709 were employed on production of building materials [*Doc. 38*].

THE NEW CAPITAL

In an attempt to westernise social life in the capital, Peter introduced 'assemblies' [*Doc. 41*] to St Petersburg after his visit to Paris. They were to be held three times a week in winter for dancing, chess, draughts and smoking, with women in attendance. Boorish though he and his male companions were, Peter decreed high standards of behaviour for these gatherings; there was, for instance, to be no heavy drinking. He had made an abortive attempt as early as 1699 to introduce women into Moscow social life by inviting them to a state dinner, but Muscovites were horrified. It is evidence of changing attitudes that it was possible to achieve this twenty years later in St Petersburg.

Inevitably a clear, but unhealthy, dichotomy opened up between the new world of St Petersburg and the vast mass of Russian society. Social tensions increased, since westernisation affected only a small part of the population. This Peter exacerbated by ordering young gentlemen to converse in a foreign language, especially in front of the servants. Upper echelons of society had already begun to use foreign terms as a form of social snobbishness, a tendency that increased markedly later in the century. Despite this, a residuum of old Russian culture remained among the upper classes, who, as children, were nursed by Russian peasant women and thus deep down retained old Russian superstitions.

Foreign influence was obvious everywhere in the new city. All technical and vocational schools in Peter's reign were directed by foreigners, drawn principally from northern Europe, The Netherlands, Germany or Britain. Peter's own particular brainchild, the Academy of Sciences, was totally foreign for many years. The new Western-style capital with its hints of Venice or Amsterdam spoke eloquently of the new Russia, just as Moscow embodied the old Muscovite past.

11 PETER'S EDUCATIONAL REFORMS

Tsar Alexis's English doctor, Samuel Collins, noted in 1671 that Russians were 'wholly devoted to their own Ignorance' and looked upon learning as 'a Monster, and fear it no less than a ship of wildfire' [43 *p. 161*]. A Saxon visitor commented on Vasily Golitsyn, chief minister under the regent Sophia: 'He was a great lover of all manner of knowledge and learning, which makes him a very strange beast indeed in Russia' [43 *p. 161*]. It would be incorrect to think there had been no intellectual activity before Peter, but it is true that until his reign there was little education except in the old church schools, where instruction was purely at an elementary level and usually confined to religious topics. At best, these institutions provided the more intelligent with tools useful for their future, but anything that smacked of the professional or practical was regarded as dangerous.

THE ACADEMIES

Certainly there had been experiments with schooling under Tsars Alexis and Feodor. A group of Ukrainian monks who arrived in Moscow in 1650 deeply influenced Simeon Polotsky, the court poet and publisher who became the protagonist of the Latinist group, but it was not until 1681 or 1682, with Feodor's approval, that his disciple, Sylvester Medvedev, founded a small Academy in the Zaikonospassky Monastery, where some twenty boys studied Latin, Greek, grammar and rhetoric [52 *p. 162*; 84 *p. 57*]. Though it was short-lived, this experiment showed the way forward by combining secular knowledge and clerical education in tandem as two branches of a single 'wisdom-science'. In the words of the 'Privilege' of 1682, by which the Academy was approved, 'We learn to know the good and bad, civil and religious affairs through a knowledge of things' [34 *p. 58*]. Under the Academy's programme the tsar was to reward diligent students of any social stratum with status, so that non-noble classes could attain higher state ranks such as *stol'nik** and *striapchii**. Scholarly education thus became the necessary precondition for state service, but ecclesiastical conservatism barred the way; reactionary elements in the church deliberately hijacked Medvedev's Academy to prevent even more radical western intrusion.

Peter was always hostile to inflexible obscurantism. He was convinced that in order to be powerful, Russia needed rapid intellectual development, with education as the mainspring of an economic, military and technological revolution. Peter's pragmatism was reflected in his educational policies. With little inclination to the arts or philosophy himself, he realised that Russia desperately needed to expand the study of subjects with immediate practical benefits, such as technology, shipbuilding, engineering, mathematics and foreign languages. In spite of all his efforts, however, he was only partially successful.

Medvedev's Academy, with its Ukrainian Latin ethos, soon found it had a rival. In 1681 Patriarch Joachim and other sponsors had set up a 'Greek' school, the so-called Typography School, with the specific aim of challenging Latinist tendencies and promoting a conservative Orthodox Greek bias. By 1686 it had 233 students. In 1685 a new Epiphany School was set up after the arrival of two Greek scholars, Ioanniki and Sofroni Likhud, who were graduates of Padua. Two years later they moved next door to Medvedev, whose smaller Latin academy thereafter failed to compete. The Slavonic-Greek-Latin (or Moscow) Academy, as it became known, took over the students from both the Epiphany and Typography Schools. The key patriarchs of Moscow and Jerusalem favoured this new Greek academy, preferring it to the Latin, and therefore suspect, ethos of Medvedev's. Ironically, within seven years this too had lost patriarchal favour. It was accused of being insufficiently conservative and went into rapid decline. However, revival was at hand. On his return from the West in 1699, brimming with ideas, Peter was appalled to discover the Moscow Academy's dilapidated state 'with its illiterate priests' and 'its 150 pupils left to their own devices' [41 *p. 164*]. Peter told patriarch Adrian that he wanted students to widen their horizons. Beyond acquiring 'a knowledge of the Gospels', they were to learn how to wage war, how to build, and how to cure the sick. Peter was later to write that 'learning is good and fundamental, and, as it were, the root, the seed and first principle of all that is useful in church and state' [48 *p. 149*]. In 1701 the tsar and Yavorskii revived the Moscow Academy, this time with an even more Latin ethos and reflecting the Ukrainian

T.C. LIBRARY, LETTERKENNY

influence which already predominated in the Russian episcopate and in contemporary church architecture. It was Ukrainians from Kiev, and not Russians, who supplied the expertise, especially in philosophy and the liberal arts, so that the Academy became the leading Russian institute of learning until Moscow University was founded in 1755. The student body itself was principally Ukrainian, Polish and White Russian.

SCHOOLS

In 1721 Peter provided the Academy with outreach beyond Moscow by establishing free diocesan schools* for which it provided the staff. By 1727 there were 46 such schools – significantly most were in the Ukraine – but standards depended on the local bishop's enthusiasm and on the availability of teachers. The best taught all the liberal arts, the remainder only grammar and rhetoric, but in true Petrine fashion they all had a practical function as providers of 'useful' state education. Though embryonic under Peter, the schools were to develop soon after 1737 into centres of secondary education for sons of priests and laity alike. The Moscow Academy's outreach into the dioceses, supported by Prokopovich, himself once Rector of the Kiev Academy, was instrumental in spreading Western Jesuit-style education, largely based on Latin models, throughout Russia.

As we have already seen, in January 1701 Peter founded the Moscow School of 'mathematical sciences and navigation' for navigators, architects and engineers. To set it in motion he recruited a Scotsman, Henry Farquharson, from Marischal College, the second university of Aberdeen, founded in 1593, and two English assistants, Stephen Gwynn and Richard Grice, from Christ's Hospital (1699). With Peter's help these three planned the school on the lines of the Royal Mathematical School at Christ's Hospital. Early progress was dogged by language difficulties, but once textbooks in Russian were available the school made rapid progress, with 400 out of the expected 500 on the roll by 1706. In 1715 Peter transferred it to St Petersburg, under the title of the Naval Academy. Though very successful, its discipline was so strict that many students fled rather than face its rigours. Retired soldiers, horsewhip in hand, were in attendance and were told 'if any pupils start to commit outrages, beat them, from whatsoever family they come' [21 *p. 102*]. Its graduates served not only as sailors, but also as engineers and architects.

Like the Moscow Academy and parallel to it, the Navigation School acted as a teachers' college by sending graduates in pairs to each province to teach arithmetic (known as 'ciphers'), geometry and grammar to the sons of landlords and officials. These 'cipher' schools* were designed to give the children of the ruling class basic education from the age of ten until they entered state service at fifteen. A completion certificate was essential for sons of the nobility if they wished to marry. The schools were, however, open to all, with free places for those from poorer homes. Nevertheless, in the long run the cipher schools tragically failed, due to Peter's impetuosity in not having the ground sufficiently prepared and parents properly motivated. The nobility and gentry withdrew their children when sons of the poor were introduced, and clergy who favoured the new diocesan schools also transferred theirs, who had hitherto made up just under 50 per cent of the intake.

The initial twelve cipher schools in 1716 grew to a peak of forty-two in 1722 with an overall total of 2,000 pupils. This number declined to 500 within two years of Peter's death, and by 1744 only eight schools remained, three of which were merged with the new garrison schools. Peter's grandiose scheme, already faltering in his lifetime, thereby met its death. Though the diocesan schools developed into seminaries, thus providing centres of secondary education for the future, Peter's dream of compulsory elementary education for all, envisaged in the cipher school system, failed. Without his vigour and awesome initiative, the momentum collapsed.

Peter sought to broaden the catchment for education in other ways. In 1714 he introduced 'free' but 'compulsory' elementary education for children of landowners and members of the civil service, who were thus to be bound to state service and receive salaries. This proved so unpopular that many escaped and Peter was compelled to revoke the edict (1716). By contrast, the foundation of further academies was successful. A school run by. Czech Jesuits between 1699 and 1705 attracted 30 well-born Moscow students. Peter's Moscow Artillery School, founded in 1701, grew from 180 students to 300 in 1704, but subsequently declined. The Moscow Medical College (1707) was followed by the Engineering College (1712) with a complement of 100 to 150, two-thirds of whom were of noble birth. The Glück Language Gymnasium, named after a Lutheran pastor from Livonia, opened in 1705 with government support to equip future diplomats with a training in politics, philosophy, literature, rhetoric, oriental and European languages.

Though it was overambitious and closed in 1715, in its time it produced 250 graduates with some proficiency in foreign languages. There were also specialist mining schools at Olonets (1716) and in the Urals (1721).

Given the circumstances, all this was a notable achievement. However, the impact of the schools was insignificant compared with the vast population. Despite Peter's avowedly broad intentions and efforts, his institutions barely touched any section of society except the gentry. Nor did moral upbringing or general education feature in his schemes. Acquisition of knowledge, not the education of the mind, was the aim; the ethos of Peter's thinking belonged to the seventeenth rather than the eighteenth century.

THE ACADEMY OF SCIENCES

Besides importing teachers from the West, Peter sent many students abroad to train as volunteers in gunnery and navigation [*Doc. 33*]. Later, others were conscripted to go abroad for training as part of state service and were paid small sums by the government. Even before his own visit to the West, Peter had sent 60 young nobles to study in Holland and Italy. From 1700 onwards the numbers increased year by year, until by 1725 an estimated 1,000 Russians had been abroad for training, at first principally to Dutch and English shipyards. Even at the beginning some nobles went abroad mainly to acquire another language, and the numbers gradually increased. In 1716 there were four studying German in Berlin and five studying Arabic and Turkish in Persia. Medicine was another skill to be acquired from the West, and in 1719 there were 30 nobles pursuing their studies of this subject abroad. Others left Russia in order to receive training in economics. The fine arts were not ignored; future painters went to Holland, architects to Italy. Many young nobles went to France – some to the Royal Academy, some as naval cadets to Toulon. Peter interviewed most on their return [*Doc. 34*], rewarded the good ones with promotion, and despatched the idlers and playboys into his kitchens or stables. The system was beneficial, in that it broadened the horizons of future diplomats, administrators and officers, and sharpened their minds. Among those who benefited was Peter Tolstoi, later Peter's shrewd envoy to Constantinople. He went to Venice at the late age of 52 to study navigation and shipbuilding, but it was the knowledge of the Italian language and Western culture which he acquired at the same time that proved useful in his diplomatic career. Another diplomat, a relative of Peter's, Prince Kurakin, also bettered himself in this way by mastering several languages that were to be useful to him as ambassador at the Hague and in Paris.

Though we cannot attribute the development in classical schools directly to Peter, the Academy of Sciences was essentially his brainchild, though it was to open only after his death [*Doc. 35*]. Aware that his drive to improve education had been only modestly successful, Peter learnt much in 1717 from his discussions at the Sorbonne and the French Royal Academy of Science, to which he was elected two years later. Leibniz, who had founded the Prussian Academy of Science in Berlin, and the prestigious German scientist, Christian Wolff of Halle, also gave advice. Peter recruited Western professors for his Academy, only for them to be surprised to discover on arrival how few students they had. To remedy this Peter's successors opened a Gymnasium in 1726, whose 120 pupils were designed to be recruits for the Academy. Though Peter did not live to see this development, and, though, ironically, it was opened by his widow, originally an illiterate peasant girl, it was his motivation which brought into being the Academy, heralded by Matthew Anderson as 'the most significant intellectual development of his reign' [38 *p. 118*]. Once established, the Academy, which still exists today, soon acquired a European reputation for both teaching and research, thus fulfilling Peter's desire that Russians should no longer be regarded 'as barbarians who hold all learning in contempt' [38 *p. 118*]. Nevertheless, it was some years before Russian members were elected to the Academy. The first 'adjunct' member took his seat only in 1733, and not until 1742 did a Russian achieve full membership.

Intellectual life flourished in other ways under Peter, especially after the Swedish danger had passed. But, even so, the motivation was still pragmatic – to improve the defence of Russia and to enhance the tsar's own authority within. Cartography naturally had a high military priority. Jan Tessing published the first maps of the Ukraine and the Black Sea neighbourhood in 1699 and by 1725 12 per cent of the empire had been mapped. The writing of recent Russian history was encouraged, in order to enhance national pride, while textbook production was increased to help to spread technology. A first Russian reading primer appeared in 1701, a Russian grammar in 1706. There were books on arithmetic, algebra, trigonometry and geometry as early as 1703, by which time Arabic numerals had already been introduced. As an aid to improved literacy the Russian script was simplified, a task in which Peter showed personal involvement even on the campaign in 1708 during Charles XII's great offensive. Printing increased rapidly and works on a multitude of technical subjects were translated into Russian – a task masterminded by Jan Tessing in Amsterdam with the help of a Ukrainian, Ilya Kopievskii.

Exploration was encouraged, since it had obvious relevance for defence, trade and the development of empire. There were expeditions to survey the vastness of the Caspian region; Siberia was explored by Daniel Messerschmitt and Titus Bering; and a new search was set underway for the north-east passage. Nor was Peter blind to the power of fine art to enhance the monarchy. As we have seen, he encouraged the circulation of engravings of Western portraits of himself. He also bought paintings through an agent in Amsterdam (1716) and sculptures from Rome. Young men were sent to Florence to study art, and Italian painters and architects were recruited to beautify St Petersburg as a capital worthy of a great power.

In one writer's words, Peter aimed to create 'a new type of Russian man, enterprising, public-spirited, open to new ideas, free from inherited prejudices' [38 *p. 124*]. In this he was partly successful, for the seeds he sowed bore fruit later in the century. But even at the time of his death, Russian intellectual and educational life was remarkably different from what it had been at his accession.

PART THREE: ASSESSMENT

12 PETER'S LEGACY

Peter died on 8 February 1725 at the early age of 52. He had a long history of strangury and stone. Decades of heavy drinking and impetuous, almost manic, activity with little relaxation had taken their toll. Indeed, the very causation of his final illness was typical. In the preceding November he had spent a whole night in the cold and wet, helping to save the lives of twenty ordinary soldiers and sailors whose boat had run aground. Characteristically, he put himself at risk to save others. It was not until 19 March that his body was taken to the cathedral of St Peter and St Paul in St Petersburg, where six years later it was finally interred. The immediate international reaction, especially among Russia's neighbours, was one of relief. There was relief too in Russia itself, for it was hoped that the heavy burdens imposed by Peter were now at an end; a fascinating satirical engraving published at the time of the funeral was entitled 'Burial of the cat by the mice' [illust. 49 p. 185; text ref. 21 p. 94]. All, however, recognised that a great man had passed. Even an English newspaper, *The Plain Dealer*, had praised Peter in May 1724 as

> the greatest monarch of our Age ... whose Actions will draw after him a Blaze of Glory, and Astonishment, through the latest Depth of Time! and warm the Heart of Posterity with the same generous Reverence for the Name of this immortal Emperor which we now feel at Mention of Alexander the Great: or the first, and noblest, of the Caesars [38 p. 169].

Prokopovich similarly eulogised Peter in his funeral address on 19 March. 'He was your Samson, O Russia ... He was your David and your Constantine, O Russian Church. ... Drawn from the paths of ignorance, our heart gives forth a sigh of relief' [38 p. 169]. One young Russian felt that Peter had 'brought our fatherland into comparison with others; he taught others to realise that we too are a people' [38 p. 169].

Russia after Peter the Great was no longer a backwater far away to the east, but an integral part of Europe. Not only did Peter make Russia predominant in the Baltic; with twenty professional diplomats in the courts of Europe he ensured that she was at the heart of the European diplomatic scene. Russia played a major part in the Austrian Succession War of 1740–48, when Russian troops reached the Rhine, and in the Seven Years War of 1756–63. She was a major beneficiary of the Partitions of Poland and subsequently a primary participant in the resistance to Napoleon. Indeed it was tsar Alexander I who was the major arbiter in Paris (1814) and Vienna (1815), where the new map of Europe, destined to last a hundred years, was drawn. In the twentieth century Russia was twice an ally of the West in resisting German domination of Europe (1914–18 and 1941–45). Russia's place as a superpower (1945–90) was but the culmination of a process begun by Ivan IV but forced at great pace by Peter.

By founding St Petersburg as a naval base, port and capital, and by conquering the vital Baltic provinces, Peter ensured Russian preeminence in the Baltic. Though temporarily lost between 1918 and 1939, the Baltic states remained part of the Russian and Soviet imperium until 1991. Russian supremacy was later enhanced by the addition of Finland (1808–1917) and the absorption of much of Poland. In Pushkin's words, Russia's entry into Europe was 'like the launching of a ship, accompanied by the knocking of axes and the roaring of cannon' [21 *p. 77*].

Peter's energetic expansion to the east and south-east, though less successful, was a blueprint for the future. He sent explorers to the Bering Straits and an expedition to the river Irtysh in search of gold, as well as emissaries to Peking. His campaigns to the Caspian against the Persians and Turks, like his expedition to gain influence over Khiva and Bukhara (1716–17), all ended in failure, but they were a prelude to later Russian expansion into Uzbekistan, Transcaucasia and Georgia. Peter would no doubt have applauded Russia's massive global influence in the mid-twentieth century. The Soviet Union's dominance of eastern Europe from 1945 to 1990 was likewise but the last phase of a movement accelerated by Peter.

In military and naval power Peter introduced a new era. By defeating Sweden overwhelmingly on land at Poltava and at sea at Hangö Udd, Peter gave Europe pause for thought. Although Russia had the long-term advantage of a much bigger population than Sweden, it was Peter's revolutionary transformation and enlargement of his army on western lines, and his creation of a fleet able to master the Baltic, that brought about such a dramatic change. Peter may have lacked the diplomatic subtleties of other statesmen, but by the end of his reign he held the essential cards in the shape of military and naval power. Though the navy declined after his death, its resurgence under Catherine II owed much to his beginnings. Russia henceforth was a power to be taken seriously in war. The military and naval power of the USSR in the mid-twentieth century could justifiably look back to Peter as its progenitor. Russian Navy Day, celebrated annually on the last Sunday of July, suitably close to the anniversary of Hangö Udd (6 to 7 August 1714 O.S.), and the Russian army's use of the Prussian goose step, introduced by Peter, are continuing reminders of his contribution.

Peter's encouragement of science and technology, fostered by the recruitment of western experts and by sending students to the West, bore fruit. The Academy of Sciences, after a slow start, began a significant Russian scientific tradition which has produced results in our own time in space technology and possibly in some aspects of medicine such as ophthalmology. Despite later Western borrowings, one historian feels that 'Peter's advancement of medicine ranks among his finest and most lasting achievements' and that he may deservedly be termed 'the father of Russian medicine' [86 in 20 *p. 208 and 194*]; medical advances were one of Peter's lasting and finest achievements.

Peter also brought about fundamental changes in the nature of the Russian monarchy. Though we should not underestimate the contributions of his predecessors, they tended to be remote, cloistered, quasi-spiritual figures. From Peter onwards tsars, like their European contemporaries, were secular monarchs with their hands on the levers of power. Instead of being a partner in government, the church was turned into a mere department of state. Like his predecessors, Peter claimed, with the patriarch, to be answerable to God alone, but by abolishing the patriarchate, his accountability to God became unique. His administrative reforms, though modified later, enabled tsars to control Russia as never before, to rule as western autocrats, hold court as monarchs and control their subjects through the *Preobrazhenskii prikaz* and the Secret Chancellery. Ivan IV had taken the title of tsar (Caesar), but Peter went further in 1721 by taking the title of Emperor (Imperator), hitherto the preserve of the Holy Roman Emperor and, at an earlier date, of the ruler of Byzantium.

Furthermore, by breaking the tsarist mystique Peter set a trend for future tsars. They may not have been so populist as Peter or fond of

Peter's simple life-style, but they were no longer semidivine. Despite his own preferences, Peter's visit to Paris caused him to follow the fashion, already current in France, of enhancing the ruler's authority through art and architecture. St Petersburg and the palaces built for him and his entourage set the tone for the future, while Alexander Nevskii's shrine added to the tsar's office historical mystique, conceptually archaic for Peter himself though it must have been. From now on, engravings of the tsar's portraits became commonplace in many noble houses.

Peter can claim some success in transforming the central organs of government. The outmoded *prikaz* system was replaced by the more successful and efficient colleges. The senate acted as vicegerent in the tsar's absence, and the Holy Synod set up to control the church outlasted his reign. At least one historian, Evgenii V. Anisimov, has eulogised the durability of these institutions [73]. It is indeed true that the collegiate system lasted until 1802, the soul-tax to 1887, the recruiting levy until 1874, the senate to 1917 and the Holy Synod to 1918. However, they bore little resemblance to the institutions Peter had created. Nineteenth-century administration owed more to Catherine than to Peter. This was particularly the case in local government, where Peter had conspicuously failed. It was left to Catherine II successfully to remodel regional and district government in 1775 and urban administration in 1785.

Economic activity developed notably during Peter's reign. The iron industry, particularly in the Urals, as well as shipbuilding and the arms industry grew apace. Indeed in iron production Russia soon led Europe (see pages 37–9). Remarkably, all this, including the building of a new fleet and a new capital, was achieved without foreign loans, but at the cost of a fivefold increase in taxation. Foreign trade with the West grew vastly, particularly through St Petersburg. Admittedly, Peter failed to develop a large-scale textile industry, but earlier historians' criticism that his trade policy was too protectionist is not valid, for he needed to guard his infant industrial economy against competition from abroad. The charge that his massive drive for industrialisation during the Great Northern War distorted the economy is also invalid. Far from economic depression after his death, there was increased entrepreneurial activity. Peter also set in motion the creation of an adequate transport infrastructure, the lack of which had been a major hindrance to economic activity. Though much remained to be done at Peter's death, the construction of a major road from Moscow to St Petersburg, the beginnings of an integrated canal network, and the creation of St Petersburg as a new and strategically significant port, all helped to provide the framework for future economic expansion.

Despite Peter's great efforts to improve education, the results were mixed. His Navigation and Mining Schools, the Engineering and Medical Colleges and the language institutes, the first specialist schools in Russia, were successful in the long run, though their impact initially on such a vast population was necessarily small. The cipher schools, intended for all, failed through lack of parental motivation and class antipathy. The diocesan schools, though more successful, lacked the technical base Peter so much needed. More auspicious was the policy of sending students to the West, and, to some extent, the import of foreign teachers. Above all, for the future, it was the creation of the Academy of Sciences, opened after Peter's death, that was to be his finest legacy in this field, though at first it was bedevilled by an inadequate 'feeder' system. In fact, Peter succeeded in sowing the seeds of secondary and technical education, which was further enhanced by the foundation in 1755 of Moscow University. However, primary education remained in the hands of the church and the army, and young nobles continued to be reliant on private tutors, just as, lower down the social scale, artisans were given a traditional training through the old apprentice system.

Peter has been chiefly criticised for creating a lasting division in Russian society between the westernised elite and the mass of Russians who remained essentially Muscovite. If this was so, it was certainly not his intention. His promotion of Western-style education for all failed in part through stiff resistance from the *boyar* class, who withdrew their children from such a socially mixed system. Westernisation certainly produced strains between the different social strata, as in twentieth-century developing nations, but it is unfair to blame Peter for failing to break the pernicious, but understandable, influence of the nobility, which his successors were to encourage in order to win support.

Peter has also been criticised for promoting too many extravagant wasteful schemes, such as, in the economic field, the canal networks of north and south, and, in the academic sphere, the Academy of Sciences before the supply of students had been assured. Nevertheless, in both of these he charted a course for the future. Others have complained that Peter did little for culture. In fact, once the threat from Sweden was over, he invited architects and artists from Italy, France and The Netherlands to build and finish St Petersburg. Works of art were bought in Amsterdam and Florence, he sponsored Western theatre, he sent artists and architects abroad and encouraged the production of works of history.

Given the colossal odds which he faced – particularly the long years of war and the conservatism of old Russia – Peter, despite all his obvious failings personal and political, deserves his place in Russian history and the title accorded him in 1721 of 'Father of the Fatherland, Peter the Great, Emperor of all Russia' [45 *p. 741*].

13 REFORMER OR REVOLUTIONARY?

Perhaps more than any other European nation, Russia has advanced not by steady evolution but by a series of leaps, interspersed with periods of stagnation and decay. Of all these phases the most startling were undoubtedly those of Peter the Great and Lenin, but Lenin's fame has been all but destroyed by the collapse of the ideology with which he was associated. Peter's, however, remains supreme as symbolised by the decision, taken in September 1991, to abandon the name of Leningrad and resort to the original one of St Petersburg.[1]

Historians have often debated the nature of Peter's reign. Was it revolutionary or not? Was he a revolutionary or a reformer? In his own time and for decades afterwards he was referred to as Peter 'the transformer', *preobrazovatel*. It was only after the French Revolution of 1789, when 'revolution' became a vogue word, that some historians looked back on Peter's reign as a period of revolution. As Alexander I. Herzen commented – in *Petr Velikii* (1851–2) – 'In Peter under the imperial purple, one senses a revolutionary' [73 *p. 296*]. Revolution implies progress towards justice and peace through coercion. In extreme form this appears in Maximilian Voloshin's poem, *Rossiya*, written in 1915 and first published in July 1917:

> Great Peter was the first bolshevik
> who plotted to overthrow Russia,
> Inclinations and morals apart,
> For hundreds of years, towards her looming distant future.
> He, like we, knew no other route,
> Except decrees, executions and dungeons,
> For the realisation of justice and truth on earth ... [73 *p. 297*]

---

[1] St Petersburg until 31 August 1914; Petrograd until 26 January 1924; Leningrad until September 1991.

In Peter, according to Mikhail P. Pogodin, a contemporary of Pushkin, writing in 1846, 'the ends of all our threads are joined in a single knot. No matter where we look, everywhere we meet ourselves in this colossal figure who casts his long shadow over all our past and even eclipses our early history. ...' [73 p. 295].

True revolution is not just progress through coercion. It should be motivated by a philosophy, a coherent system of thought, as in the French revolution of 1789, the Leninist revolution of 1917, and Mao's revolution in China. In Peter's reforms, however, this was not the case. It might be thought that in borrowing from the West ideas of monarchy, Erastianism, administration, economics and social custom he was revolutionary, but in fact Peter at all times thought 'on the hoof', at least in his early years; all was manically pragmatic, with the aims of saving Russia from foreign threats, enhancing the monarch's power, and making an entry on to the European stage with a resounding crash. If he behaved as a common man, Peter did so because he enjoyed it and to set an example, not as part of a revolutionary egalitarian ideal.

Revolution also implies a break with the past, yet, as a modern Russian historian, Evgenii V. Anisimov, has written (1989 trans. 1993), Peter's 'revolution ... possessed a distinctly conservative character. Modernisation of the institutions and structures of authority for the conservation of the fundamental principles of the traditional regime appeared to be the ultimate aim. We are discussing the emergence of the autocratic rule that lived on until the late 20th century' [73 p. 298]. This process entailed the intensification of tsarist and *boyar* control over the serfs and the extension of tax and service burdens on the serfs.

In some fields Peter accelerated changes, albeit drastically, that were already taking place. His military reforms had been prefigured by the earlier Romanovs, including Tsar Alexis, who had brought in Western troops of 'the new formation'. It was the speed and intensity of Peter's reforms in this field that were so new.

Ivan IV had already opened up trade routes with the West and the iron works at Tula in the 1630s, but this was but a prelude to the breakneck economic developments under Peter. Even the celebrated enforcement of state service on the nobility, crystallised in the Table of Ranks, was not entirely new. Under previous monarchs there had been compulsory state service and a complex ranking system, known as the *mestnichestvo*. Peter replaced this with an ordered system of precedence based on service, where everyone, no matter what was their social background, had to start from the bottom.

Peter also inherited an administrative system built round departments, the *prikazy*; but these overlapped in their functions and were inefficient. Peter's collegiate system, by contrast, was revolutionary in its concept. For Asinimov, Peter's major contribution was to introduce 'statism' into Russia [73 *p. 296*], but if this was indeed the case, subsequent generations of Russian and Soviet citizens had to pay a terrible price for it.

What was entirely new, entirely Peter's achievement, was the navy. Landlocked as Muscovy had been, Russians had no experience of, nor indeed love for, the sea. Peter's decision to build a mighty navy of 850 warships to dominate the Baltic was indeed revolutionary. His assumption of direct control over the church, which he turned into a department of state with the clergy as his agents, in place of the traditional partnership between Church and Crown, was again revolutionary, in line with the most extreme western forms of Erastianism. St Petersburg itself was revolutionary in both concept and design. It symbolised Peter's turning away from 'holy Russia' in his determination to free himself and the monarchy from the shackles of the past. The same was true of his insistence on the adoption of western fashions of dress and beard shaving.

In summary, Peter was revolutionary in a number of ways, but generally speaking he 'sharply intensified the processes under way in the country; he forced it to make a gigantic leap, carrying Russia all at once through several stages that she inevitably would have to traverse sooner or later' [73 *p. 298*].

PART FOUR: DOCUMENTS

DOCUMENT 1   FIRES IN MOSCOW 1698

Johann Korb was the secretary to the Holy Roman Emperor's ambassador in Moscow. He describes everyday life there soon after his arrival. Fires were common.

May 6. Another fire gave us cause to tremble. It is a consequence of the constant orgies [in this case Easter] of the populace. For the greater the feast the larger is the measure of their potations. ... Hardly any great festival of the year passes without being followed by a conflagration. These fires are all the more disastrous because they mostly break out at night time; and sometimes they utterly consume to ashes some hundreds of wooden houses. Some of the Germans [i.e. foreigners] who had run to put out the last fire, by which 600 houses were devoured on this side of the river Neglina, being falsely accused of theft, were, after being most atrociously flogged, cast into the flames and immolated to the fury and recklessness of this people. ...

Diary of an Austrian Secretary, [9], p. 101.

DOCUMENT 2   THE EMPEROR'S ENVOY HAS AN
AUDIENCE WITH THE TSAR
13 SEPTEMBER 1698

September 13. At four in the afternoon we went with a most splendid train to audience. It took place in the magnificent house which the Czar had built at his own cost and presented to his general and admiral, Lefort. Numbers of magnates were around his majesty, and amidst them all the Czar stood pre-eminent with a handsome figure and lofty look that bespoke the latent monarch. ... We made our reverential obeisances which his majesty acknowledged with a gracious nod which augured kindness. ... The Czar graciously took them [the letters credential] and then admitted the Lord Envoy and all the officials of the embassy and the missionaries [i.e. envoys] present, to kiss hands. ...

Diary of an Austrian Secretary, [9], p. 161.

DOCUMENT 3   PETER THE MASTER SHIPWRIGHT

10 December 1709

After noon I set off for the Admiralty wharf to be present at the raising of the stem of a 50-gun ship, but on that day was raised only the forestem, because the derricks proved to be too weak to raise the stem. The tsar, as the chief shipwright (a post for which he receives a salary), supervised everything, took part in the work along with the others and, where necessary, swung an axe, which he wields more skilfully than all the other carpenters there.

Just Juel in Evgenii V. Anisimov, [73], p. 21.

DOCUMENT 4   IMPRESSION ON PRINCESS SOPHIA OF HANOVER, 11 AUGUST 1697

The Great Embassy
a) In Hanover 1697

The Tsar is very tall, his features are fine, and his figure very noble. He has great vivacity of mind, and a ready and just repartee. But, considering all the advantages with which nature has endowed him, it could be wished that his manners were a little less rustic. ... He was very merry, very talkative, and we established a great friendship for each other, and he exchanged snuff-boxes with my daughter. We stayed, in truth, a very long time at table, but we would gladly have remained there longer still without feeling a moment of *ennui*, for the Tsar was in very good humour, and never ceased talking to us. My daughter had her Italians sing. Their song pleased him, though he confessed to us that he did not care much for music.

I asked him if he liked hunting. He replied that his father had been very fond of it, but that he himself, from his earliest youth, had had a real passion for navigation and for fireworks. He told us that he worked himself in building ships, showed us his hands, and made us touch the callous places that had been caused by work. ...

He is a very extraordinary man. It is impossible to describe him, or even to give an idea of him, unless you have seen him He has a very good heart and remarkably noble sentiments. I must tell you, also, that he did not get drunk in our presence, but we had hardly left, when the people of his suite made ample amends.

Evgenii V. Anisimov, [73], p. 18.

DOCUMENT 5

b) Amsterdam 1697

The writer, John Perry, was recruited by Peter in England in 1698 and worked as an engineer in Russia until 1712.

Most commonly when he [Peter} came to a seaport he went about in a Dutch skipper's habit, that he might go among the shipping and be the less taken notice of. ... The magistrates [in Amsterdam] ... had prepared for him a very magnificent house for his residence. But the Czar having taken a particular fancy and resolution on his own part to learn the art of shipbuilding ... chose to take a small house on the East-India wharf (or shipyard) just by the waterside, where there were strict orders given, that neither any mob from abroad, nor the people in the yard, should gaze and disturb him; a thing he was the most averse to imaginable. Here he lived for some months, with two or three of his favourites, whom he took to be partners with him in learning the art of shipbuilding. He wrought one part of the day with the carpenter's broad ax among the Dutchmen; and for the better disguise wore the same sort of habit which they did: And at other times diverted himself with sailing, and rowing upon the water.

P. Putnam, [12], pp. 29–30.

DOCUMENT 6

c) London 1698

Peter borrowed John Evelyn's house where he and his companions made a poor impression. Evelyn's servant writes to him:

There is a house full of people, and right nasty. The Czar lies next your Library, and dines in the parlour next your study. He dines at 10 o'clock and 6 at night, is very seldom at home a whole day, very often in the King's Yard, or by water, dressed in several dresses. ...

John Evelyn's Diary, [3], p. 284 note.

Peter left England on 21 April and Evelyn himself later noted:

9 [June 1698]. ... I went to Deptford to view how miserably the Tzar of Moscovy had left my house after 3 moneths making it his Court, having gotten Sir Cr: Wren his Majesties Surveyor & Mr. London his Gardener to go down & make an estimat of the repairs, for which they allowed 150 pounds in their Report to the L: of the Treasury. ...

John Evelyn's Diary, [3], p. 290.

DOCUMENT 7

He made a better impression on Gilbert Burnet, Bishop of Salisbury, who writes to Dr. James Fall, Precentor of York, later archdeacon of Cleveland.

...the Czar came oure to Lambeth and saw both an Ordination and a Sacrament and was much pleased with it. I have been oft with him. On Monday last I was four hours there. we went thro many things. he has a degree of knowledge I did not think him capable of. he has read the Scriptures carefully. He hearkned to no part of what I told him more attentively than when I explained the authority that the Christian Emperours assumed in matters of Religion and the Supremacy of our Kings. I reassured him that the question of the Procession of the H[oly Ghost]† was a subtilty that ought not to make a Schism in the Church. He yielded that Saints ought not to be praied to and was only for keeping the Picture of Christ, but that it ought only to be a Remembrance and not an object of worship. I insisted much to shew him the great designs of Christianity in the Reforming of mens hearts and lives which he assured me he would apply himself to. He grows so fond of me that I hardly get from him. ... The Czar will either perish in the way or become a great man ... Gi: Sarum

19 March 98

† A reference to the difference in theological doctrine between Eastern and Western churches over the so-called *Filioque* clause – as to whether the Holy Spirit proceeds 'from the Father' (Eastern) or 'from the Father and the Son' (Western) – a point of difference since the Middle Ages.

Bodl. MSS. Add. D23, [2], f.10.

Burnet to Fall 19 March 1698.

DOCUMENT 8   PETER DEMONSTRATES HIS SKILL IN
              WOODWORK

Peter at his second (official) wedding to Catherine brings his own handmade sconce [i.e.candle-bracket] 20 February 1712 (they had been secretly married since 1707). Charles Whitworth was the British ambassador (see Document 10).

Prince Menschikoff carried the marshall's staff, and vice-admiral Cruys was in the sled with the Czar, at his right hand, as his father,[†] His Majesty left his sled with some impatience a little before they came to the door, that he might have time to hang up a sconce with six branches of ivory and ebon-wood, which he had turned himself, and then placed it in the middle of the room over the table. He told me it had cost him about a fortnight's time and no-one else had touched it; the piece is indeed curious for the workmanship, as well as the hand that made it. ...

Letter of Charles Whitworth, [13], p. 145.

[†] i.e. for the wedding ceremony.

DOCUMENT 9   PETER WRITES TO HIS WIFE, CATHERINE

Carlsbad 14 September 1711. Katerinushka, my friend, how art thou? We arrived here well, thank God, and tomorrow begin our cure. This place is so merry, you might call it an honourable dungeon, for it lies between such high mountains that one scarcely sees the sun. Worst of all, there is no good beer. However, we hope God will give us good from the waters. I send thee herewith a present, a new-fashioned clock, put under glass on account of the dust, and a seal. ... I couldn't get more on account of my hurry for I was only one day in Dresden.
    Altona 23 May 1716. Katerinushka, my heart's friend how are you? Thanks for the present. In the same way I send you something from here by return. Really on both sides the presents are suitable. You sent me wherewithal to help my old age and I send you with which to adorn your youth.
    Altona 23 November 1716. ... Alexander Petrovitch writes that Petrushka[†] has cut his fourth tooth, God grant he cut all so well and that we may see him grow up, thus rewarding us for our former grief over his brothers...;

L. J. Oliva, [11] p. 67–68.

[†] The future Tsar Peter II.

DOCUMENT 10   **THE ENGLISH AMBASSADOR ARRIVES**

Charles Whitworth was English Ambassador to Russia from March 1705 (O.S.) to April 1710 and October 1711 to June 1712. After the Act of Union with Scotland (1707) he would have been known as the British – not English – ambassador.

11 March 1705/6

On the 19th Febr: I set out from Smolensko having been furnished by the waywede [i.e. *voevod*] or governor with horses for my baggage and a Major with 12 soldiers being appointed for my Convoy. ...

at the end of the Suburbs I found the Stolnik* waiting with 11 Coaches and a great retinue. He alighted first to make me a Compliment, and then we proceeded in the following manner (1 ... [the coaches listed in order] ... (3 4 of the Czaars own Coaches in the last whereof I sat with the Pristaff [i.e. an official] and Interpreter, and was attended by 6 footman ... (7 The waggons and sleds which brought my baggage – and in this formality I was carried ... [to] the town a[t] footspace, and severall stops being made, it was above 4 hours before I got to a Palace in the Duch [i.e. German or foreign] suburb built by the late Generall Lefort, where a very handsome apartement had been provided and a Lieutenant with 36 soldiers appointed for my guard.

at my coming in, I found a present from the Czaar which consisted in wine mead, Brandy and other refreshments. The streets thro' which I passed were filled with all sorts of people and I was brought thro' 7 of the triumphal arches which had been erected for the Czaar at his return from the Campagne and are still standing, but what I admired the most was to see no one of any fashion appear in a Russian habit, being all dressed after the German manner. The next morning I had a privat audience from the Czaar in the house of his first Minister where I was very oblidgingly received and presently after his great favourit Alexander visit[ed], and the Chief Minister, Feodor Alexiowitz Gollovin, has since made me the same compliment.

I am with respect, My Lord,
yr Lordps most obedient humble servant
C. Whitworth

Letter of Charles Whitworth, [1], ff. 6–7.

DOCUMENT 11   THE POLTAVA CAMPAIGN:
THE IMPROVEMENT IN RUSSIAN
MILITARY SKILL

James Jefferyes, an Englishman born in Sweden (1679-80), served from January to October 1719 as ambassador in St Petersburg. Earlier, being fluent in Swedish, he served as a volunteer in the Swedish army under Charles XII, though clandestinely as a diplomat reporting regularly to London. He served throughout the campaign in Russia, was captured at Poltava, but on release he became English emissary to Charles XII at Bender.

[JEFFERYES TO SECRETARY OF STATE , WHITEHALL]

[1 September 1708 O.S. Wolownika]

The Svedes must now own the Muscovites have learnt their lesson much better than they had either at the battles of Narva or Fraustadt, and that they equall if not exceed the Saxons both in discipline and valour, 'tis true their cavalry is not able to cope with owrs, but their infantry stand their ground obstinately, and 'tis a difficult matter to separate them or bring them in a confusion if they be not attacked sword in hand; nevertheless 'tis most probable they will not hazard a battle with us, but endeavour by surprises and by cutting of owr provisions to moulder away owr army, which is very practicable in this country, where the inhabitants having burried their provision quitt their houses, and the ennemy burn whatever they come over. ...

Letter of James Jefferyes, [8], p. 59.

DOCUMENT 12   PETER'S ADDRESS BEFORE THE BATTLE
OF POLTAVA

Let the Russian host know that that hour has come that places the fortunes of our entire Fatherland in their hands: either to perish utterly or for Russia to be reborn in a better condition. And let them not think that they were armed and put forth for Peter, but for the state entrusted to Peter, for their kin, for the Russian people. ... As to Peter, they should know clearly that his life is not dear to him, provided only that Russia lives, Russian piety, glory and well-being. ...

from N. I. Pavlenko, *Petr Pervyi 169* N. V. Riasanovsky, [35] p. 9.

DOCUMENT 13   THE DEFEAT AT POLTAVA: THE BRITISH
AMBASSADOR'S VIEW

Mosco 6/17 July 1709

My Lord
The unexpected defeat of the wholle Swedish army before Pultava and the
dispersing of their Troops has been so great, that the news thereof will
certainly come to your hands before this letter. However I would not fail to
let you know what His Czarish Majesty has writ to his Ministers on this
glorious occasion from his camp the 27th of June O.S.

> This morning very early the Enemy with his wholle army, Horse and
> Foot, attack'd our Horse, who having behaved themselves very well a
> considerable time, and done great Execution were at last oblig'd to retire,
> but formed themselves agin in both wings of our foot, which was drawn
> up in Battle at the Head of our Camp; this the Swedes observing formed
> themselves also in a Line against our front and begun a second attack,
> but were so well received, that they were immediately beat out of the
> field with very little loss on our side; wee have taken a great many
> Colours and pieces of canon with Feld-Marshall Reinschield, four Major-
> generals ... and some thousand officers and soldiers; the particulars of
> which we cannot as yet get together; In a word the wholle army has met
> with Phaetons[†] Destiny. as to the King of Sweden wee cannot yet tell if
> he is kill'd or amongst the prisoners. ...

> ...This great Victory will probably give a new change to all the affairs of
> the North and King Stanislas is like to find the first effects, the Czar being
> resolved to march into Poland. ... I shall be now curious to see what
> resolution King Augustus will now take. I still beleive he onely waited for
> the troubling of the Waters, and perhaps will now step in first.
> I am with all respect,
> [1] BL. Add 31128. ff. 170–3.

Letter of Charles Whitworth, [1], ff. 170–3.

[†] In classical mythology Phaeton, the son of Phoebus (the Sun), undertook to drive
his father's chariot which he upset with disastrous consequences.

DOCUMENT 14　POLTAVA: AN ENGLISHMAN WITH
　　　　　　　　CHARLES XII WRITES

[JEFFEREYES TO SECRETARY OF STATE, WHITEHALL
13 July 1709 O.S. Pultava.]

Right Honourable,

...Y:r Hon:r understood by my last of the 12:th inst. that the Svedes have
had an entire defeat by Pultava; that 14:m [i.e. 14,000] ... yielded
themselves prisonners of warr, and that the King of Sveden made his escape
over the Nieper with 2 or 3000 as well officers and soldiers for Poland.
This strange reverse of fortune has wholy chang'd the face of affairs in these
parts, the Moscovites who have an army of 100:m [i.e. 100,000] men a foot
are now ready to enter Poland, the infantry as I am informed is to march to
Liefland probably to besiege Riga while their cavalry advances towards
Lemberg without doubt to raise new factions against the Svedes in Poland
and to renew King Augusts right to that crown; ... Y:r Hon:r ... will best be
able to judge whether these projects are consistent with the balance Her
Maj:ty and Her glorious predecessors have allways maintain'd among the
Princes of Europe. ...

I am etc.

Pultava July the 13:th O.S.

1709

endorsed:
　M:r Jeffreys Pultawa
　July 13. O.S. 1709
　Recd Sep: 7

Letter of James Jefferyes, [8], p. 76–7.

DOCUMENT 15 THE PEACE OF PRUTH 1711

Letter from Jefferyes 27 July 1711 from Bender

[Russian envoys] ... being admitted to the Grand Vizir* and returning soon afterwards to the camp, Monsr Shaffirow, vice-chancellor to the Czar, and Feltmarchall Czeremetofs son were dispatched thither, where they remain'd the whole night, and where a peace was clapt up the 13th in the morning, ... the conditions of which are, that Azof shall be delivered to the Turks in the condition it was when the Muscovites took it; that Taganrock, Samara and Kamiensaton should be demolish'd, but all the ammunition that is in Kamiensaton shall be delivered to the Turks, and the Muscovites shall never pretend to build any fortification in that place for the future; that the Czar shall not molest or injure the Poles, the Cossacks of Ukrain or those of Zitsh, but shall suffer them to remain in their former .state and condition; that the Russian Merchants shall have free commerce to Constantinople as heretofore; that the Czar shall have no Ambassadr henceforth at Constantinople; that all the Turks who are made prisoners by the Muscovites shall be set at liberty; that the King of Sweden (who is a friend and guest of the Emperour) shall not be hindred by the Czar to return to his own dominions and that the Ottoman Port should be glad to see the differences between them adjusted; that the Vizir shall entreat the Emperour to ratify this treaty; that Monsr Shaffirow and young Czeremetof shall remain as pledges by the Grand Vizir. ...

These articles being agreed to by the Czar, the Muscovite army march'd out of their prison the 14th in the afternoon with their swords drawn, drums beating, collours flying, with cannon and baggage, having ... 1500 Turks to conduct them to the boarders. But their army was in so bad condition that most of their Cavalry went on foot and the greatest march they could make was not above 2 hours or a mile a day. 'Tis thought that the loss which the Czar sustain'd in this expedition amounts to upwards of 20^m [i.e. 20,000] men. ...

Letter from James Jefferyes, [5], p. 11.

DOCUMENT 16 PEACE NEGOTIATIONS
RUSSIAN ACTIVITY DURING THE ÅLAND
PEACE NEGOTIATIONS

James Jefferyes to the right honourable secretary of state.
Reval, July the 30th o. s. 1719.

The reports we have of His Czarish Majesty's progress against Sweden are so various and uncertain...; we have been amused some days past with the news of a proposal said to be made by the swedes of a cessation of arms; now we are told that the moscovites are advanced to within 4 leagues of Stockholm and that they have attacked and made themselves masters of two swedish fortresses; ... The letters of the 17th only confirm that His Czarish Majesty, with some of his gallies, had been to take a view of Wexholm (which lies ... but 4 leagues from Stockholm). ...

Letter of James Jefferyes, [13], p. 570.

DOCUMENT 17 **THE PEACE OF NYSTAD 1721**

In the name of the Very Holy and Indivisible Trinity, be it known by this treaty that, as there has been carried on for several years a bloody, long and difficult war between His Majesty the dead King Charles XII, of glorious memory, King of Sweden, ... and his successor to the throne of Sweden, Ulrica, Queen of Sweden ... and, on the other hand, His Czarist Majesty Peter I, Emperor of all Russia the two parties have found the means to conclude these troubles and consequently put an end to the shedding of so much innocent blood. ...

Article I. There will be from this moment and forever an inviolable peace on land and a sincere, friendly and indissoluble union between His Majesty King Frederick I, King of Sweden, etc., his successors to the crown and the Kingdom of Sweden, and all his domains, provinces, cities, vassals, subjects and inhabitants, and His Czarist Majesty Peter I, Emperor of all Russia, etc., his successors to the throne of Russia, and all his provinces, cities, vassals, subjects and inhabitants. ... In the future the two peaceful parties will not commit, nor permit to be committed, any secret or public, direct or indirect hostility either by themselves or by others. They will give aid to no enemy of either of the two peaceful parties under any pretext whatever and will make no alliance which would be contrary to the peace. ...

Article IV. His Majesty, the King of Sweden, by the present articles, cedes ... to His Czarist Majesty and his successors in the Russian empire, in full, irrevocable and eternal possession, the provinces which have been conquered and taken by the arms of His Czarist Majesty in this war against the crown of Sweden. That is to say: Livonia, Estonia, Ingria and part of Karelia as far as the district of Vibourg ... the cities and fortresses of Riga, Dunemund, Pernau, Reval, Dorpat, Narva, Vibourg, Kexholm, and other cities, fortresses, ports, places. districts, coasts and rivers pertaining to the said provinces, as also the isles of Oesel, Daghoe, Moen and all the other islands along the frontier of Courland and along the coasts of Livonia, Estonia, and Ingria, and on the western side of Reval, ...

Article V. His Czarist Majesty promises His Majesty and the crown of Sweden in return to restore and to evacuate within four weeks after the exchange of ratifications of this peace treaty, or sooner if possible, the Grand Duchy of Finland, except the part which has been reserved below in the boundary details, which will belong to His Czarist Majesty. ...

Article VII. His Czarist Majesty also promises, in the manner most solemn, that he will not mingle in the domestic affairs of the Kingdom of Sweden nor the form of regency which has been regulated and established unanimously by the estates of the foresaid Kingdom; ...

Article IX. His Czarist Majesty promises to maintain all the inhabitants of the provinces of Livonia, Estonia, and Oesel, nobles and free peasants, magistrates and artisans, in the entire enjoyment of the customary privileges and prerogatives which they have enjoyed under the rule of the King of Sweden.

Article X. One will not introduce restraints of conscience in the countries which have been ceded, but one will allow and maintain the evangelical religion as well as the churches and the schools and their dependencies on the same footing as they were in the time of the last regency of the King of Sweden, on the condition that the Greek religion is also freely exercised.

Made at Nystad, August 30th, 1721.

L. J. Oliva, [11], p. 56–8.

DOCUMENT 18   **LACK OF RUSSIAN ENTHUSIASM: PETER EXPRESSES HIS FRUSTRATION**

(From a *ukaz* of 1723)

...Either our decrees are not accurately observed, or there are few people who wish to go into the business of manufacturing. ... That there are few people wishing to go into business is true, for our people are like children who never want to begin the alphabet unless they are compelled by their teacher. It seems very hard to them at first, but when they have learnt it they are thankful. So in manufacturing affairs we must not be satisfied with the proposition only, but we must act and even compel, and help by teaching, by machines and other aids, and even by compulsion, to become good economists. For instance, where there is fine felt we should compel people to make hats, by not allowing the sale of felt unless a certain number of hats are made.

B. H. Sumner, [48], pp. 162–3.

DOCUMENT 19 LACK OF RUSSIAN ENTHUSIASM: AN ENGLISH ENGINEER'S VIEW

...Secondly, In case of any number of men being sent from the places where they live to go upon any of the Czar's works, if any artificers are more ingenious than their fellow-workmen, unless it be where the Czar himself is present and takes cognisance of it they have oftentimes more labour and care of work committed to their charge, but have no encouragement given them for their ingenuity more than another man. When I was at Veronize [i.e.Voronezh], I order'd a Dutch master carpenter who was under my command, upon occasion of an engine that was to be made, to chuse out two or three of the most ingenious persons that he could find among the Russ carpenters to be employ'd in it;...

And notwithstanding all that I could do by the representations I have made ... to have some small encouragement to be given to such as I found deserving out of the Czar's treasure, yet I could never obtain so much as one single copeek a day encouragement for any one person; it being not the manner of Russia, on any such works as I was employ'd on to pay any money or wages at all to common artificers and labourers out of the Czar's treasure.

...Upon these considerations, it is no great wonder that the Russes are the most dull and heavy people to attain to any art or science of any nation in the world ... the Czar, where he is present does indeed give encouragement to some of those common artificers and workmen, who have the happiness to be under his eye, and whom he finds deserving. ... But his boyars are quite of another temper ... and the generality of his subjects remain still under the same check and discouragement to ingenuity.

P. Putnam, [12], pp. 59–61.

DOCUMENT 20 THE BRITISH AMBASSADOR – WITH A DIFFERENT VIEW – FORECASTS THE GROWTH IN RUSSIAN NAVAL STRENGTH 1719

James Jefferyes who had served under Charles XII (see Document 11) was British ambassador to St Petersburg between January and October 1719. Perry (see Document 19) had left Russia in 1712

...I now beg leave to entertain your lordship with another set of people, who because the Czar greatly favours them, have got here the nickname of chips by those that envy them, but by others are called ship-builders; these in my humble opinion (if continued long in this service) will not fail of setting the Czar on such a footing as will enable him to bid fair for mastery in the East-sea [i.e. the Baltic]. One of them assured me lately that if the Czar lives three years longer, he will have a fleet of forty ships of the line from seventy to ninety guns each, as good as any the world can afford, besides twenty frigats from thirty to forty cannon each, all built at this place; these people the Czar flatters and caresses as much as possible; their salaries are large and punctually paid, they eat in private with him, they sit at his table in the greatest assemblies, and he hardly goes anywhere or takes any diversion but some of them accompany him. By these caresses the Czar means to captivate their affections...

Letter of James Jefferyes, [13], p. 515.

DOCUMENT 21   THE PRODUCTION OF RUSSIAN IRON

OUTPUT OF PIG IRON 1718–1735 (in metric tonnes)

Year	State	Private	Total
1718	3,636	5,635	9,271
1719	3,622	5,518	9,140
1720	2,539	7,435	9,992
1721	2,752	7,453	10,205
1722	3,125	9,831	12,957
1723	2,233	8,316	10,549
1724	5,012	7,699	12,711
1725	4,717	8,633	13,350
1726	3,586	8,634	12,220
1727	3,472	7,912	11,384
1728	5,025	9,390	14,415
1729	6,185	8,485	14,670
1730	5,307	10,369	15,676
1731	6,323	13,039	19,362
1732	6,387	10,780	17,167
1733	5,962	11,483	17,445
1734	6,421	13,530	19,953
1735	7,198	15,758	22,950

W. L. Blackwell, [51], p. 376.

TRADE WITH GREAT BRITAIN (IN £)

TRADE OF RUSSIA WITH GREAT BRITAIN

Year	Russian Exports	Russian Imports	Excess of Exports
1715	241,876	105,153	136,723
1716	197,270	113,154	84,116
1717	209,898	105,835	104,064
1718	284,485	79,626	204,869
1719	140,550	55,295	85,255
1720	169,932	92,229	77,704
1721	156,258	95,179	61,079
1722	112,467	54,733	57,734
1723	151,769	56,697	95,072
1724	212,230	35,564	176,666
1725	250,315	24,848	225,468
1726	235,869	29,512	206,357
1727	144,451	21,883	122,568
1728	232,703	25,868	206,835
1729	156,381	35,092	121,289
1730	258,802	46,275	212,527
1731	174,013	44,464	129,549
1732	291,898	49,657	242,241
1733	314,134	42,356	271,778
1734	298,970	36,532	262,438
1735	252,068	54,336	197,732

W. L. Blackwell, [51], p. 373.

R.T.C. LIBRARY, LETTERKENNY

DOCUMENT 22   **KORB DESCRIBES WORK IN A PRIKAZ 1698**

20 May. In the public offices which the Muscovites call Prikass, the chief clerk is called Ali. His duty is to watch constantly that the rest actively pursue their work. One day the business was so great, that it was considered necessary to give up the whole night as well as the day to it, though only the day was paid for. Ali had in consequence betaken him to rest. The remaining mob of scribblers followed his example. The day after, the Dumnoi [i.e. state councillor or secretary], becoming aware of the contumacy of the clerks condemned Ali to receive in proper person, the penalty of the battok – a kind of cudgelling – as being the prime offender, by the very bad example he had given the rest by contempt of orders. The clerks, after the manner of outrageous criminals, were chained with iron to their places, and fettered, to teach them how to write night and day.

The Diary of an Austrian Secretary, [9], p. 110.

DOCUMENT 23   A COMPARISON BETWEEN RUSSIAN AND
SWEDISH SYSTEMS OF COLLEGES

*Heinrich Fick's knowledge of the Swedish system was vital for the plans for
the Russian colleges. Instructions were often copied verbatim. This is just
one of several examples.*

SWEDISH *INSTRUKTION* (1694)

RUSSIAN INSTRUCTIONS (1719)

His Royal Majesty's ordinance, by which the tasks of his *kammarkollegium* are to be distributed among the members of the college for the promotion of prompt expedition.

His Tsarist Majesty's most gracious ordinance, according to which the tasks (*otpravlenie*) of his *kamerkollegiya* are to be distributed among its members for the promotion of a rapid expedition.

Given at Stockholm, 25 May a:o 1694

Given at St Petersburg.

Since the quantity, importance, and prolixity of treasury affairs and the problems connected with them demand not only time, but also care to be dealt with well and clearly, ...; but it seems possible not only to facilitate and forward the work in a remarkable way, but also to avoid much confusion and disorder, if a certain method is applied and, for the second thing, a certain distribution among the members of the college is carried out as to the most important and most difficult tasks of the college, that is, when it comes to the method, too; thus His Royal Majesty wishes to have it in general ordained.

Since the quantity, importance and extent of the treasury affairs and the problems which derive from them demand not only time, but also care if they are to be dealt with clearly and thoroughly [and]..., not only much relief and help for the work can be gained, but also many mistakes and disorders can be avoided, if in the first place a certain way is used for this, and in the second place a certain distribution of the most important and difficult tasks is made among the members of the college, thus it pleases His Tsarist Majesty to ordain in the following manner.

C. Peterson, [82], p. 170–1.

DOCUMENT 24 TOWN GOVERNMENT: THE *RATUSHA* 1699

The *ukaz* of January 30

It has come to the attention of the high monarch, that [the merchants] have suffered great losses in their commerce and trade and have been ruined by the procrastination (*volokita*) of the *prikazy*, so that some of them have abandoned their commerce and trade and become poor, and from this the state and ordinary incomes have suffered a loss, and the extraordinary imposts [have suffered] great shortages. And so that they, the town people (*posadskie liudi*), shall not suffer procrastination and losses in the various *prikazy* and be ruined, and so that the high monarch's treasury – the direct taxes – shall not suffer shortages and the indirect imposts shall not only not come in undiminished, but shall also increase, therefore the high monarch has shown them his benevolence and decreed: in future the urban population of Muscovy, when it comes to their judicial cases and their taxes, shall no longer lie under the jurisdiction of the *prikazy*, where they formerly lay, but rather the *burmistry* [i.e. the members of the *Ratusha*, translator's note] shall administer the town people throughout the Muscovite realm. –

C. Peterson, [82], p. 148.

DOCUMENT 25 FICK'S VIEW ON ADEQUATE SALARIES AS A DEFENCE AGAINST CORRUPTION 1718

First and foremost, each realm must support its officials in an honourable manner and according to need, as we can see happen in all Christian realms, [and] Russia has received from the highest grace in nature greater advantages with which to support her officials than has Sweden; secondly, it is better to give 100 roubles in salary than to allow 200 or 300 roubles in fraud; thirdly, there is no realm which loses a single rouble by paying a million roubles in salary if all this money is expended within the realm again; fourthly, we can never convince clever subjects to accept service in this state unless they are driven to it by the hope of salary and promotion.

C. Peterson, [82], p.98.

DOCUMENT 26 THE TABLE OF RANKS, 24 JANUARY 1722

Military Ranks		*Civilian Ranks*	*Grades*
Naval Forces	*Land Forces*		
General-Admiral	Generalissimo Field Marshal	Chancellor or Active Privy Counsellor	I
Admiral	General of Artillery General of Cavalry General of Infantry	Active Privy Counsellor	II
Vice Admiral	Lieutenant General	Privy Counsellor	III
Rear Admiral	Major General	Active State Counsellor	IV
Captain-Commander	Brigadier	State Counsellor	V
First Captain	Colonel	Collegial Counsellor	VI
Second Captain	Lieutenant-Colonel	Court Counsellor	VII
Lieutenant-Captain of the Fleet Third Captain of Artillery	Major	Collegial Assessor	VIII
Lieutenant of the Fleet Lieutenant-Captain of Artillery	Captain or Cavalry Captain	Titled Counsellor	IX
Lieutenant of Artillery	Staff Captain or Staff Cavalry Captain	Collegial Secretary	X
		Secretary of the Senate	XI
Midshipman	Lieutenant	*Guberniya* Secretary	XII
Artillery Constable	Sublieutenant	Registrar of the Senate	XIII
	Guidon Bearer	Collegial Registrar	XIV

TABLE OF RANKS – RULES

The following rules are appended to the above Table of Ranks to inform everyone how he should apply himself to these ranks.

...2. Naval and land commanding officers are to be determined in the following manner: if they are both of the same rank, the naval officer is superior at sea to the land officer, and on land, the land officer is superior to the naval officer, regardless of the length of service each may have in his respective rank.

8. Although We allow free entry to public assemblies, wherever the Court is present, to the sons of princes, counts, barons, distinguished nobles, and high servants of the Russian state, either because of their births or because of the positions of their fathers, and although We wish to see that they are distinguished in every way from other [people], We nevertheless do not grant any rank to anyone until he performs a useful service to Us or to Our state. ...

11. All Russian or foreign-born servants who have or who have had the first eight grades have the right forever to pass these grades on to their lawful heirs and posterity. ...

15. Those who are not nobles but who serve in the military and who advance to ober-officer [position] will, upon attainment of that rank, receive the status of a nobleman, ...

L. J. Oliva, [11], p. 52–3.

DOCUMENT 27 **THE DRUNKEN SYNOD**

Korb describes the frolics of the Drunken Synod

February 21. [There were] a sham Patriarch and a complete set of scenic clergy dedicated to Bacchus, with solemn festivities at the palace which was built at the Czar's expense and which it has pleased him now to have called Lefort's. A procession thither set out. ... He that bore the assumed honours of the Patriarch was conspicuous in the vestments proper to a bishop. ... Cupid and Venus were the insignia on his crosier, lest there should be any mistake about what flock he was pastor of. The remaining rout of bacchanalians came after him, some carrying great bowls of wine, others mead, others again beer and brandy, that last joy of heated Bacchus.

Diary of an Austrian Secretary, [9], p. 255.

DOCUMENT 28 **THE SPIRITUAL COLLEGE: PART OF THE OATH OF MEMBERS**

Again, I swear by Almighty God that I resolve, and am in duty bound, to be a faithful, good, and obedient slave and subject to my natural and true Tsar and Sovereign, Peter the First, Autocrat of All Russia, etc.; and after him, to Their Highnesses, the legitimate Heirs of His Tsarist Majesty ... and to Her

Majesty, Our Sovereign, Tsaritsa Ekaterina Aleksieevna. All the rights and prerogatives (or privileges) which have been enacted and will be enacted into law, appertaining to the high sovereignty, power, and authority of his Tsarist Majesty, I will defend and guard to the utmost of my knowledge, strength, and opportunity, and in this I will not spare my life, if occasion demands. ... As for whatever concerns damage, harm, or loss to His Majesty's interests, as soon as I become aware of it, I will not only inform of it in due time, but will strive by all possible means to avert it and not to tolerate it.

A. V. Muller, [10], p. 6.

DOCUMENT 29 PRIESTS AS INFORMERS: INSTRUCTIONS IN THE SUPPLEMENT TO THE SPIRITUAL REGULATION 1722

11. If someone in confession informs his spiritual father of some illegality that has not been committed, but that he yet intends to commit, especially treason or mutiny against the Sovereign or against the state, or evil designs upon the honour or well-being of the Sovereign and upon His Majesty's family, and in informing of such a great intended evil, he reveals himself as not repenting but considers himself in the right, does not lay aside his intention, ... When the spiritual father, in God's name, enjoins him to abandon completely his evil intention, and he, silently, as though undecided or justifying himself, does not appear to have changed his mind, then the confessor must ... expeditiously report concerning them, where it is fitting, pursuant to His Imperial Majesty's personal ukase, promulgated on the twenty-eighth day of April of the present year, 1722, which was published in printed form with reference to these misdeeds, in accordance with which it is ordered to bring such malefactors to designated places, exercising the greatest speed, even as the result of statements concerning His Imperial Majesty's high honour and damaging to the state. Wherefore a confessor, in compliance with the provisions of that personal ukase of His Imperial Majesty, must immediately report, to whom it is appropriate, such a person who thus displays in confession his evil and unrepentant intention. ... But in that report (sic) shall only be stated secretly that such a person, indicating therein his name and rank, harbours evil ideas and impenitent intent against the Sovereign ... therefore he must be apprehended and placed under arrest without delay.

A. V. Muller, [10], p. 60–1.

DOCUMENT 30 EXPULSION OF THE JESUITS MAY 1719. THE BRITISH AMBASSADOR WRITES

I send your lordship here inclosed translated copies of His Czarish Majesty's declaration posted up at this place [St Petersburg] and at Moscow, ordaining all the jesuits who are under the emperor's protection to depart forthwith out of this country, and because they are a set of people who commonly entertain correspondence abroad and often intermeddle in affairs that do not belong to them, their papers have been seized and examined which I suppose will be restored to them before their departure; they are to be conducted from hence as far as Mitaw ... the shortness of time will not permit me to send your lordship any other translation than this german and an italian one, which I think is pretty well done, and will be fully understood by your lordship.

Jefferyes to Stanhope, [13], p. 531. (1 May 1719)

DOCUMENT 31 PETER WRITES TO ALEXIS

My Son:

Your disobedience and the contempt you have shown for my orders are known to all the world. Neither my words nor my corrections have been able to bring you to follow my instructions and, last of all, having deceived me when I bade you farewell and in defiance of the oaths you have made, you have carried your disobedience to the highest pitch by your flight and by putting yourself like a traitor under a foreign protection. ...

I write to you for the last time to tell you that you are to do what Messrs Tolstoy and Rumyantsov will tell you and declare to be my will. If you are afraid of me, I assure you and I promise to God and his judgement that I will not punish you. If you submit to my will by obeying and if you return, I will love you better than ever. But if you refuse, then I as your father, by virtue of the power I have received from God, give you my everlasting curse; and as your sovereign, I declare you traitor and I assure you I will find the means to use you as such, in which I hope God will assist me and take my just cause into his hands.

As for what remains, remember I forced you to do nothing. What need had I to give you a free choice? If I had wished to force you, was it not in my power to do it? I had but to command and I would have been obeyed.

Peter

Letter to Tsarvich Alexis 1717
R. K. Massie, [45], p. 687.

DOCUMENT 32   THE CONDEMNATION OF ALEXIS

The Czarevich ... has made himself unworthy of the clemency and pardon which was promised to him by his lord and father. He has said so himself before His Czarist Majesty and in the presence of all the ecclesiastics and secular lords and publicly before all assembled. ...

... The Czarevich contemplated a horrible double parricide against his lord: first against the father of his country and second against his own natural father, a very clement father who has raised the Czarevich since his infancy with the most paternal care and with a tenderness and a goodness which have always been recognised. The father tried to educate the son for government, and to instruct him carefully in the important military arts, in order to make him capable and worthy of succession to such a great empire. ...

... It is with an afflicted heart and tearful eyes that we, as servants and subjects, pronounce this sentence ... against the son of the great and most clement sovereign Czar, our lord. However, his will being that we make a judgement, we declare by this present decree our true opinion and we pronounce his condemnation with a conscience so pure and so Christian that we believe we can sustain it before the terrible, just, and impartial judgement of the great God. We submit this sentence ... to the merciful revision of His Czarist Majesty, our very merciful monarch.

L. J. Oliva, [11], p. 64–5.

DOCUMENT 33   AN INSTRUCTION TO RUSSIAN STUDENTS ABROAD STUDYING NAVIGATION

1. Learn [how to draw] plans and charts and how to use the compass and other naval indicators.

2. [Learn] how to navigate a vessel in battle as well as in a simple manoeuvre, and learn how to use all appropriate tools and instruments; namely, sails, ropes and oars, and the like matters, on row boats and other vessels.

3. Discover as much as possible how to put ships to sea during a naval battle. Those who cannot succeed in this effort must diligently ascertain what action should be taken by the vessels that do and those that do not put to sea during such a situation [i.e. naval battle]. Obtain from [foreign] naval officers written statements, bearing their signatures and seals of how adequately you [Russian students] are prepared for [naval] duties.

4. If, upon his return, anyone wishes to receive [from the Tsar] greater favours for himself, he should learn, in addition to the above enumerated instructions, how to construct those vessels aboard which he would like to demonstrate his skills.

5. Upon his return to Moscow, every [foreign-trained Russian] should bring with him at his own expense, for which he will later be reimbursed, at least two experienced masters of naval science. They [ie the returnees] will be assigned soldiers, one soldier per returnee, to teach them [what they have learned abroad]. And if they do not wish to accept soldiers they may teach their acquaintances or their own people. The treasury will pay for transportation and maintenance of soldiers. And if anyone other than soldiers learns [the art of navigation] the treasury will pay 100 roubles for the maintenance of every such individual

L. J. Oliva, [11], p. 50.

DOCUMENT 34   THE SERVICE STUDENT: PETER THE
                EXAMINER

On the 30 June a *prikaz* ordered us to appear for an examination on July 1, being reunited at the College, we were waiting for instructions. At 8 a.m. the Sovereign arrived in a ramshackle cart and as he passed he said 'Hail, children!' After this we had to enter the assembly and the Admiral-general ordered Zmievic to question us one by one what each knew about navigation. When my turn came ... the Sovereign deigned to approach me and without letting Zmievic put his questions asked me: 'Have you learnt all for which you have been sent?' To which I replied: 'Most merciful Sovereign, I have applied myself with all my power, but I cannot pride myself on having learnt everything and I appear before you an unworthy slave and for that I beseech, as from God, your mercy'. As I said these words, I knelt and the Sovereign resting his right hand on my palm, gave me it to kiss and deigned to say to me: 'You see, brother, I am the Tsar, and I have blisters on my hands and all that to this end: to give you an example and at least in my old age to see around me contributors of merit and servants of the nation.' Still on my knees I took his hand myself and kissed it several times and he said to me: 'Arise, brother, and answer what you will be asked, but do not be afraid, if you know something say it, if you do not know it, the same. ...'

Taken from 'Zapiski' (Memoires of Nepljuev 1718)
S. Blanc, [4], p. 55 (translated).

DOCUMENT 35   THE FOUNDING OF THE ACADEMY OF
SCIENCES. A DECREE. 28 JANUARY 1724

His Imperial Majesty decreed the establishment of an academy wherein
languages as well as other sciences and important arts could be taught and
where books could be translated. On January 22 [1724] during his stay in
the Winter Palace, His Majesty approved the project for the Academy, and
with his own hand signed a decree that stipulates that the Academy's budget
of 24,912 rubles annually should come from revenues from custom dues
and export-import licence fees collected in the following cities: Narva,
Dorpat, Pernov and Arensburg. ...

5 ... what is needed most in [Russia] is the establishment of an institution
that would consist of the most learned people, who, in turn, would be
willing: (a) to promote and perfect the sciences while at the same time,
wherever possible, be willing (b) to give public instruction to young people
(if they feel the latter are qualified) and (c) instruct some people individually
so that they in turn could train young people [of Russia] in the fundamental
principles of all science.

7. Because the organisation of this Academy is similar to that of Paris
(except ... that the Russian Academy is also to do what a university and
college are doing (in Paris)), I think that this institution can and should
easily be called an Academy. Disciplines ... can easily be grouped in three
basic divisions: The first division is to consist of mathematical and related
sciences; the second of physics; and the third of humanities, history and law
... .

L. J. Oliva, [11], pp. 53–5.

DOCUMENT 36   ST PETERSBURG – THE TSAR LAYS A
FOUNDATION STONE, 1706

*The English Ambassador, Charles Whitworth, comments on the vulnerability of
the new city and reports on the beginning of new fortifications.*

Mosco 19/30 June 1706

... Before the Court left Petersburg [for Cronschloss and Narva on 31
May], the Swedish fleet consisting of 15 men of war appeared before that
harbour, but only kept cruising in the sea, at about 10 or 15 English miles
distance, without making show of any other attempt.
On the 30th May O.S. being the Czar's birthday, His Majesty laid the
first stone of the fortifications at St Petersburg being a square marble,

ingraved with his name, the day and year; and all his Court assisted at his Ceremony: All the Bastions are to be built of free stone to prevent the dammadge of the spring flood. ...

Letter of Charles Whitworth, [1], pp. 46–7.

DOCUMENT 37   ST PETERSBURG – WHITWORTH
DESCRIBES PROGRESS BY 1712 AND
DISCUSSES TRANSPORTATION PROBLEMS

On this place the Czar has fixed his point of view, and designs to raise a town for the residence of the merchants, which in a few years is to equal Amsterdam in its wealth and beauty, and to be the Venice of the north, in which the trade of all Russia is to center. The plan is already drawn for seven thousand brick houses, with a little yard to each, large warehouses and squares in the principal places, which are to take up the whole island, the chief streets being to be cut through with canals as in Holland; and because the sea has often overflowed great part of it in the autumn, a digue [embankment] is to be raised and carried quite round. ...

As to the climate, here it is seldom above six months frost; in the summer, it is true, the winds are often high, and then runs a very hollow sea in the narrows especially when a strong gale sets in ... and forces the waters of the Baltic into the gulph, which will make the passage troublesome for small boats, and often disappoints the inhabitants since most of what they use in their housekeeping must be brought from the opposite shores.

The whole country of Ingria is not fruitful in itself, and ... the chief supplies of every sort now come from Moscow, as well as the merchandise must hereafter, and therefore, a communication has been long aimed at between the lake of Ladoga and the banks of the river Wolga [i.e. Volga]. ... About three years ago a canal was cut between the two rivers not far from Novgorod, by which a small brigantine was brought hither from Kazan after a passage of two years. ... The last year one captain Perry, an englishman, was employed [in finding a shorter route] ... and he thinks he has found out a place where by cutting a canal across the country near twenty english miles and setting up about twelve sluices, a communication might be made for bringing timber, corn and all other goods from Kazan in three or four months, which would be a great advantage to the Czar, especially for his fleet, there being plenty of noble oak about the Wolga, and not a stick for the service in all this country.

Letter of Charles Whitworth 17 June 1712, [13], pp. 225–7.

DOCUMENT 38   ST PETERSBURG – THE WORKFORCE

Friedrich Christian Weber arrived in St Petersburg as Hanover's ambassador in 1714. An admirer of Peter, he wrote extensive memoirs during his seven years in Russia. He did not approve of all he saw.

'... the orders were forthwith issued, that next Spring [1703] a great number of Men, Russians, Tartars, Cosacks, Calmucks, Finlandish and Ingrian Peasants, should be at the Place to execute the Czar's Design. Accordingly in the beginning of May 1703, many thousands of Workmen, raised from all Corners of the vast Russian Empire, some of them coming Journies of 200 to 300 German Miles, made a beginning on the Works on the new Fortress. There were neither sufficient Provisions for subsisting such a number of men, nor Care taken to furnish them with the necessary Tools, as Pick-axes, Spades, Shovels, Wheelbarrows, Planks and the like, they even had not so much as Houses or Huts, notwithstanding which the Work went on with such Expedition, that it was surprising to see the Fortress raised within less than five Months time, though the Earth which is very scarce hereabouts, was for the greater part carried by the Labourers in the Skirts of their Clothes, and in Bags made of Rags and old Mats, the Use of Wheelbarrows being then unknown to them. It is computed that there perished on this Occasion very nigh one hundred thousand Souls, for in those Places made desolate by the War, no Provisions could be had even for ready Money, and as the usual Supplies carried by the Lake Lagoda were frequently retarded by contrary Winds, those People often were in the utmost Misery. ...

F. C. Weber, [14], Vol. I pp. 299–300.

DOCUMENT 39   ST PETERSBURG – SOME BUILDING REGULATIONS BY *UKAZ*, 1714

1. On the City Island and the Admiralty Island in St Petersburg, as likewise on the banks of the greater Neva and its more important arms, wooden buildings are forbidden. ... The two above mentioned islands and the embankments excepted, wood may be used for buildings, the plans to be obtained from the architect Trezzini. The roofs are to be covered either with two thicknesses of turf laid on rafters with cross-ribs (not on laths or boards) or with tiles. No other roof covering is allowed under penalty of severe fines. The streets should be bordered directly by houses, not with fences, or stables.

2. ... Whereas stone construction here is advancing very slowly, it being difficult to obtain stone-masons and other artisans of this craft even for

good pay; for this reason all stone buildings of any description are forbidden in the whole state for a few years, until the construction has sufficiently progressed here, under the penalty of confiscation of the offenders' property and exile. ...

3. The following is ordered: no building shall be undertaken in St Petersburg on the grounds of houses, between neighbouring backyards, until all the main and side streets are entirely built up. ... No stables or barns may be built facing the street. ... Along the streets and side streets all must be filled with residences, as ordered. In the locations where, as ordered by previous decrees, wooden houses may be built, they must be made of squared logs ... the walls must be faced with boards and coated with red or painted to look like brick.

L. J. Oliva, [11], p. 45.

DOCUMENT 40   ST PETERSBURG – ITS UNPOPULARITY

John Perry describes the feelings of the nobility before his departure in 1712.

The Czar obliges [the nobility] against their will, to come and live at Petersburgh ... where they are oblig'd to build new houses for themselves, and where all manner of provisions are usually three or four times as dear, and forage for their horses, etc, at least six times as dear as it is at Mosco; which happens from the small quantity which the countrey thereabouts produces, being more than two thirds woods and bogs. ... Whereas in Mosco, all the lords and men of distinction, have not only very large buildings within the city, but also their countrey seats and villages, where they have their fishponds, their gardens, with plenty of several sorts of fruit and places of pleasure; but Petersburgh, which lies in the latitude of 60 degrees and 15 minutes north, is too cold to produce these things. Besides, Mosco is the native place which the Russes are fond of, and where they have their friends and acquaintance about them; their villages are near, and their provision comes easy and cheap to them, which is brought by their slaves ... when they get together by themselves, they complain and say that there are tears and water enough at St Petersburgh, but they pray God to send them to live again at Mosco.

P. Putnam, [12], p. 61–2.

DOCUMENT 41   ST PETERSBURG – SOCIAL LIFE.
REGULATIONS FOR HOLDING ASSEMBLIES
AT PETERSBURG, 1718

Enthused by his visit to Paris (1717), Peter tried to introduce western-style social life. Here he lays down the minutiae of how assemblies should be conducted.

Assembly is a French term which cannot be rendered in a single Russian word. It signifies a number of persons meeting together either for a diversion or to talk about their own affairs. ... After that manner we will have those assemblies kept maybe learned from what follows:

1. The persons at whose house the assembly is to be in the evening to hand out a bill or other sign to give notice to all persons of either sex.

2. The assembly shall not begin sooner than four or five in the afternoon, nor continue later than ten at night.

3. The master of the house is not obliged to go and meet his guests, to conduct them out, or to entertain them; but, though he himself is exempt from waiting on them, he ought to find chairs, candles, drink and all other necessaries asked for, as also to provide for all sorts of gaming and what belongs thereto. ...

4. No certain hour is fixed for anybody's coming or going; it is sufficient if one makes his appearance at the assembly.

5. It is left to everyone's liberty to sit walk or play, just as he likes, nor shall anybody hinder him or take exception at what he does. ... As for the rest, it is enough to salute at coming and going.

7. A particular place shall be assigned to the footmen (those of the house excepted) that there may be sufficient room in the apartments designed for the assembly (that is, so that the rooms would not be clogged with footmen hanging about and mingling with the guests).

R. K. Massie, [45], p. 808–9.

GENEALOGY: THE ROMANOV DYNASTY

Michael
(b. 1596)
1613–45

|
Alexis m. (2) Natalia Naryshkina
1645–76 (d. 1694)
(b. 1629)

Maria Miloslavskaya (1) m.
(d. 1669)

Sophia **Feodor III** **Ivan V** m. Praskovia   Evdokia Lopukhina (1) m. **Peter I** m. (2) **Catherine I**   Natalia
Regent 1682–69 1676–82 1682–96 Saltykova   (d. 1731)   1682–1725   1725–27   (b. 1673 d. 1716)
(b. 1657 d. 1704) (b. 1661) (b. 1666) (d. 1723)   (b. 1672) (b. 1684)

Charles-Leopold   Alexis   m.   Charlotte   Charles Frederick   m. **Anna** **Elizabeth**   Peter
Catherine m. Duke of Mecklenburg-   (b. 1690)   of Brunswick-   Duke of Holstein-   (d. 1728) 1741–62   Petrovich
(d.1733)   Schwerin   (d. 1718)   Wolfenbüttel   Gottorp (d. 1739)   (b. 1709)   (b. 1715)
              (d. 1747)   (d. 1715)   (d. 1719)

           Anna   m.   Anton-Ulrich   **Peter II**   **Peter III** m. Sophia of Anhalt-Zerbst
           Regent   Prince of   1727–30   1762   who became
           1718–46   Brunswick-Bevern   (b. 1715)   (b. 1728)   **Catherine II**
           (b. 1718, d. 1764) (d. 1776)   1762–96
                                                                                         (b. 1729)

                Ivan VI   **Paul**
                1740–41   1796–1801
                (b. 1740, d. 1764)   (b. 1754)

                                                                              Alexander I **Nicholas I**
                                                                              1801–25   1825–55

                                                                                        Alexander II
                                                                                        1855–81

                                                                              Alexander III
                                                                              1881–94

                                                                              Nicholas II
                                                                              1894–1917

The names of rulers are given in bold type, with their dates of rule.

GLOSSARY

archimandrite – the head of a Russian Orthodox monastery.

ascribed labour – the distinctively Russian practice of 'ascribing' groups of villages to the service of particular factories, both state and privately-managed.

bayonet – plug bayonets replaced pikes in the West in the 1690s, followed by the more effective ring bayonet in the 1700s.

black peasants – descendants of the original Asiatic non-Slav population of Muscovy.

boyar – the highest rank of hereditary landed nobility.

Boyarskaya Duma – the assembly of *boyars* which fell into disuse under Peter the Great.

chin – a service title conferring social rank.

chinoproizvodstvo – system of uniform ranking and career development, established under the Table of Ranks.

cipher schools – schools started under Peter the Great for the teaching of mathematics.

corvolant – a special corps of light cavalry, introduced by Peter the Great, i.e. a mixture of light cavalry, light infantry and light artillery.

Cossacks – bands of irregular cavalry, Orthodox by religion, who escaped the rule of old Muscovy, but had colonised the Upper Ukraine.

diocesan schools – set up in 1721 in each diocese and staffed by teachers from the Moscow Academy.

doli – literally 'fractions'. Local government areas, introduced in 1715, divided according to exact population size.

dragoons – light mobile cavalry.

Dukhovnyi Reglament – the *Spiritual Regulation*, the key legislation for church reform, proclaimed in a manifesto of 25 January 1721 with a Supplement of June 1722.

dvorianstvo – the nobility.

Erastianism – a system whereby the Church is subject to the secular power, as in Lutheran and Anglican states.

fiskal – (plural *fiskaly*) an official under the Senate, drawn from the lower orders or foreigners, whose duty was to search out inefficiency.

flintlock – introduced for muskets in the late seventeenth century as an improvement on the previous methods of powder ignition.

foreign formation – see 'new formation' below.

frigate – a medium-sized square-rigged warship.

galley – a shallow-draught vessel powered by oars, common in the Mediterranean from Roman times and in the Baltic during Sweden's rise to ascendancy.

Gallicanism – a term asserting the autonomy of national Catholic churches, especially in France, while still recognising the Pope's spiritual primacy.

generaletit – the senior four ranks in the Table of Ranks.

Generalprokuror – the tsar's official who presided over the Senate.

glavnyi magistrat – the government department ('Chief Magistracy') set up in 1721 to supervise Russian towns.

Gordonovskii – named after General Patrick Gordon, it was one of the four regiments of guards. Originally one of Peter's 'toy regiments'.

Great Russia – (or Muscovy) the large part of the original land of the Rus based on Moscow. Called 'Great' because it had twelve dioceses as opposed to Little Russia's five.

guberniya – (plural *gubernii*) an area of local government, created by Peter in 1708.

hetman – the title of the ruler of the Cossacks.

khan – title of a Mongol ruler.

knout – a hard thong of leather about three-and-a-half foot long fixed to a stick two-and-a-half foot long, used for interrogation and punishment, sometimes with the victim suspended with arms tied behind his back.

kollegiya – (plural *kollegii*) one of the government departments established by Peter in 1718.

Latiniser – a derogatory term used by Russian conservative ecclesiastics for an advocate of reforming the Russian Church along western lines.

Lefortovskii – named after General Lefort, it was one of the four regiments of guards. Originally one of Peter's 'toy regiments'.

Little Russia – The Ukraine (see below), based on Kiev. So-called originally by the Patriarch* of Constantinople because it had only five dioceses as opposed to Great Russia's twelve.

liturgy – a form of church worship. The Liturgy is the normal Orthodox term for the Mass or Eucharist.

mercantilism – a seventeenth/eighteenth century economic theory which stated that a nation's wealth depended on its possession of precious metals, so that trade surplus and protection of home industries were of great importance.

mestnichestvo – the complicated old Muscovite system of precedence, abolished in 1681–2.

Metropolitan – a senior archbishop in the Orthodox church, but less important than the patriarch.*

monastyrskii prikaz – the monastery department. The government department set up in 1701 to control church finances.

Most Drunken Synod – made up of his drinking companions, this was Peter's parody of the church.

Muscovy – the name normally used for Russia until the late seventeenth century. Also called Great Russia.

Nemetskaya Sloboda – the foreign or 'German' suburb of Moscow established for foreigners in 1652. The translation of Nemetskii is dumb, so literally Nemetskaya Sloboda, means 'dumb suburb'.

'new formation' (*novogo stroya*) regiments – first created in 1631, on western lines, they were the main element in the army from the 1670s onwards.

oberfiskal – a senior official overseeing the duties of the fiskals.

patriarch – the senior Orthodox prelate in a region or country.

poll-tax (or 'soul-tax') – Peter's tax on individuals raised in 1724.

pomeshchiki – landholders owing the Tsar military service for land.

pood – a unit of weight. About 36 lbs.

Porte – the government of the Ottoman Empire.

poteshnie polki – the so-called 'toy regiments' formed by Peter in his youth.

posolskii prikaz – the foreign affairs department under the old *prikaz* system.

Preobrazhenskii prikaz – originally in the 1690s the office which administered the Preobrazhenskii regiment. Subsequently, it assumed responsibility for public order in Moscow and, eventually, for suppressing political opposition throughout Russia.

Preobrazhenskii regiment – named after Preobrazhenskoe (see below), it was one of the four regiments of guards. Originally one of Peter's 'toy regiments'.

Preobrazhenskoe – a village outside Moscow near the German suburb favoured by tsar Alexis and where Peter spent his childhood.

prikaz – (plural *prikazy*) a government department before Peter's reforms.

raskolniki – literally 'schismatics'. Normally applied to the 'Old Believers' (*starovertsy*) who refused to recognise the ecclesiastical reforms of patriarch Nikon.

ratusha – established in 1699 by Peter as a central organ for town government (esp. Moscow).

reketmeister – an official first appointed in 1722 to investigate complaints about the working of the *kollegii*.

rekrut – recruit, conscripted from 1705 onwards. Significantly a western word instead of the earlier term *datchnynye lyudi*.

Rus – the early name for the Russian people after the legendary Rurik. It crystallised into the three Russias – Great (Muscovy), Little (Ukraine), White (see below) during Mongol times.

Secret Chancellery – (*tainaya kantsellariya*) a government agency set up at St Petersburg initially to investigate the case against tsarvich Alexis.

Semenovskii regiment – named after the village of Semenovskoe, it was one of the four regiments of guards. Originally one of Peter's 'toy regiments'.

ship-of-the-line – a warship with at least 60 guns.

soul-tax – see poll-tax.

starovertsi – the Old Believers. See under *raskolniki*.

stol'nik – a table attendant.

striapchii – a crown agent.

streltsy – a corps of about 50,000 hereditary and privileged troops originating in the late sixteenth century. The name originates from *strelets* (a shooter). By the late seventeenth century they were hostile to change.

Tatars – a largely nomadic people, Muslim descendants of the Mongols.

tsar – the title (Caesar) first taken by Ivan IV in 1546.

uezd – (plural *uezdy*) a local government district between 1708 and 1715.

ukaz – a decree issued by the tsar.

Ukraine – the part of the original land of the Rus based on Kiev. From the sixteenth century it was under Polish rule and thus became Poland's frontier (*ukrainia*). Subject to western influence. Also called Little Russia.

Ulozhenie – the new law-code of 1649.

ultramontane papalism – a seventeenth-century western term for centralised papal authority, as distinct from Gallicanism.*

uniates – a church created in Poland in 1596. It retained Orthodox liturgy, but accepted papal authority.

ustav voinskii – the Military Regulations of 1716.

vizier – the chief minister of the Sultan in the Ottoman Empire.

voevod – (plural *voevody*) a provincial governor before Peter's reforms.

White Russia – part of the original land of the Rus. It fell under Lithuanian rule in the fifteenth century and was thus subject to western influence. The origin of the name 'white' is unclear.

Zaporozhian – name given to the Cossacks who lived on islands in the river Dnieper 'below the rapids' (*za porogi*).

Zemskii Sobor – the Assembly of Land, a representative body in Muscovy made up of representatives of the service class and town merchants. It declined in power in the seventeenth century.

TOPOGRAPHICAL GLOSSARY

Names traditionally used in historical works in this area may not be found on modern maps. The following list will help the modern traveller who is also a student of the period to locate the places of interest.

Historical name	Alternative name
Åbo (Swedish)	Turku (Finnish)
Åland	Ahvenanmaa (Finnish)
Danzig (German)	Gdansk (Polish)
Dorpat	Tartu (Estonian)
Hangö Udd (Swedish)	Gangut (Russian) Hanko (Finnish)
Holowczyń (Polish)	Golovchin
Lesnaya (Russian)	Lesna (Polish)
Nystad (Swedish)	Uusikaupunki (Finnish)
Reval	Tallinn
Stanelishte	Stanilesti
Viborg (Russian)	Viipuri (Finnish)
Wexholm	Vaxholm

1. *Russia in 1725*

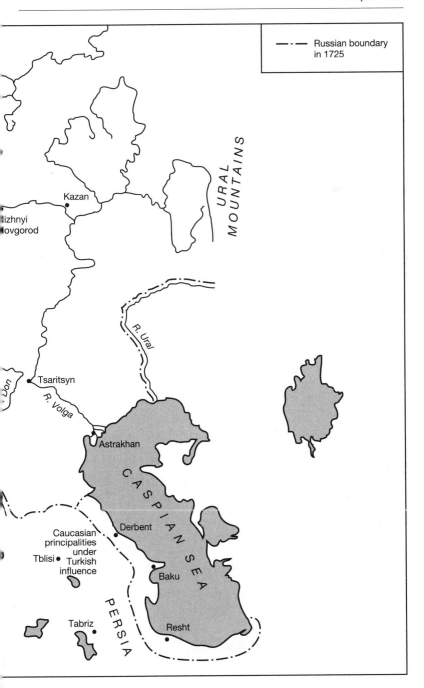

Russian boundary
in 1725

URAL MOUNTAINS

Kazan

Nizhnyi
Novgorod

R. Ural

Don

Tsaritsyn

R. Volga

Astrakhan

C A S P I A N   S E A

Caucasian
principalities
under
Tblisi ● Turkish
influence

Derbent

Baku

P E R S I A

Tabriz

Resht

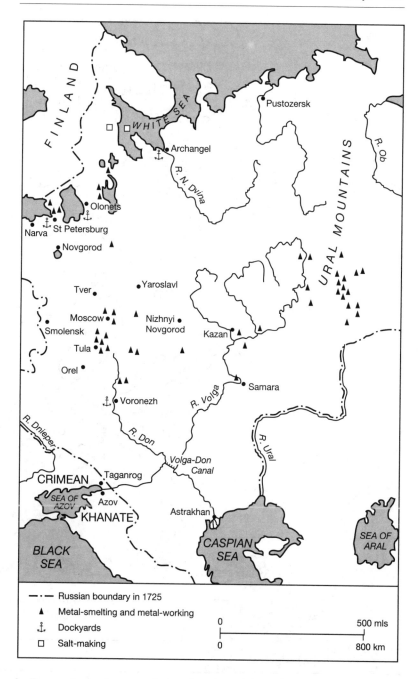

2. *Economic development during the reign of Peter the Great*

3. *Military campaigns and revolts under Peter the Great*

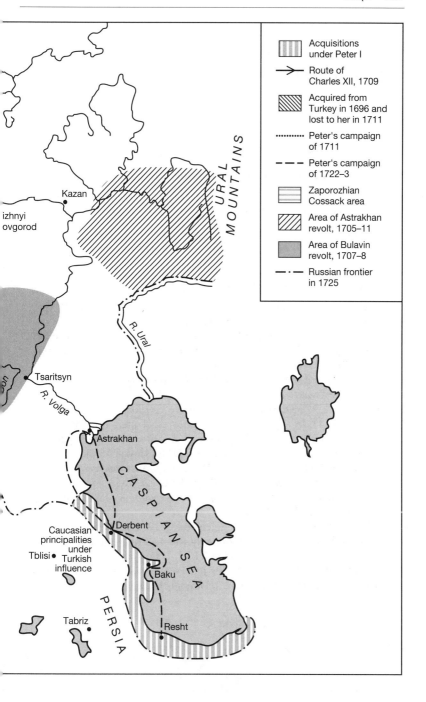

Acquisitions
under Peter I

Route of
Charles XII, 1709

Acquired from
Turkey in 1696 and
lost to her in 1711

Peter's campaign
of 1711

Peter's campaign
of 1722–3

Zaporozhian
Cossack area

Area of Astrakhan
revolt, 1705–11

Area of Bulavin
revolt, 1707–8

Russian frontier
in 1725

Kazan

izhnyi
ovgorod

URAL MOUNTAINS

R. Ural

Tsaritsyn

R. Volga

Astrakhan

CASPIAN SEA

Derbent

Caucasian
principalities
under
Tblisi • Turkish
influence

Baku

PERSIA

Tabriz

Resht

BIBLIOGRAPHY

The place of publication is London, unless otherwise stated.

PRIMARY SOURCES: MANUSCRIPT

1   BL Add MS 31128 Letters of Charles Whitworth 1705–1709.
2   Bodleian Add. D23.10 Letter of Bishop Burnet to James Fall 1698.

PRIMARY SOURCES: PRINTED

3   Beer, E. S. de (ed.)*The Diary of John Evelyn*, 6 vols, Oxford, 1955.
4   Blanc, S., *Pierre le Grand*, Paris, 1974.
5   Carlsen, E. (ed.), Letters of Captain James Jefferyes from the Swedish Army 1711–1714 in *Historiska Handlingar rorande Skandinaviens historia*, no. 16.2, Stockholm, 1897.
6   Cracraft, J. (ed.), *For God and Peter the Great: The Works of Thomas Consett 1723–29*, New York, 1982.
7   Gordon, P., *The Diary of General Patrick Gordon 1635–1699*, 1968.
8   Hatton, R. H. (ed.), Captain James Jefferyes's Letters from the Swedish Army 1707–1709, published in *Historiska Handlingar rorande Skandinaviens historia*, no. 35, Stockholm, 1953.
9   Macdonnell, Count (tr. and ed.), *Diary of an Austrian Secretary of Legation at the Court of Czar Peter the Great*, 1863.
10   Muller, A. V. (tr. and ed.), *The Spiritual Regulation of Peter the Great*, Seattle, WA, 1972.
11   Oliva, L. J., *Peter the Great*, Englewood Cliffs, NJ, 1970.
12   Putnam, P., *Seven Britons in Imperial Russia*, Princeton, NJ, 1952.
13   *Russian Historical Society Archives LXI*. Letters of Charles Whitworth 1711–19, and James Jefferyes 1719. St Petersburg, 1888.
14   Weber, F. C., *The Present State of Russia*, 1723.

SECONDARY SOURCES: BOOKS
General

15   Anderson, M. S., 'Russia under Peter the Great and the changed relations of east and west' in 18.

16 Anderson, M. S., *Europe in the Eighteeenth Century 1713–1783*, 1961.
17 Black, J., *Eighteenth Century Europe 1700–1789*, 1990.
18 Bromley, J. S. (ed.), *The New Cambridge Modern History Vol VI. The Rise of Great Britain and Russia. 1688–1715/25*, Cambridge, 1970.
19 Cherniavsky, M., *Tsar and People*, New Haven, CT, 1961.
20 Cracraft, J. (ed.), *Peter the Great Transforms Russia*. 3rd edition, Lexington, MA, 1991.
21 Dukes, P., *The Making of Russian Absolutism, 1613–1801*, 1982.
22 Florinsky, M. T., *Russia: A History and an Interpretation*, 2 vols, New York, 1953.
23 Garrard, J. G. (ed.), *The Eighteenth Century in Russia*, Oxford, 1973.
24 Kliuchevsky, V. O., *A Course in Russian History: The Seventeenth Century*, ed. A. J.Rieber, tr. N. Duddington, Chicago, 1968.
25 Kubitjovyc, V., *Ukraine: A Concise Encyclopedia*, Toronto, 1963.
26 Lewitter, L. R., 'Peter the Great and the Modern World' in *History Today*, vol. 35 (February 1985).
27 Maland, D., *Europe in the Seventeenth Century*, 1967.
28 Miliukov, P. N., *History of Russia*, New York, 1968.
29 Munck, T., *Seventeenth Century Europe 1598–1700*, 1990.
30 Oakley, S. P., *War and Peace in the Baltic 1560–1790*, 1992.
31 Pennington, D. H., *Seventeenth Century Europe*, 1972.
32 Philipp, W., 'Russia: the Beginnings of Westernisation' in F. L. Carsten (ed.), *The New Cambridge Modern History: The Ascendancy of France 1648–88*, Cambridge, 1961.
33 Previte-Orton, C. W., *The Shorter Cambridge Mediaeval History*, Cambridge, 1966.
34 Raeff M., *Peter the Great. Reformer or Revolutionary?* Boston, 1963.
35 Riasnovsky, N. V., *The Image of Peter the Great in Russian History and Thought*, New York, 1985.
36 Rothstein, A., *Peter the Great and Marlborough*, New York, 1986.
37 Young, I., 'Russia' in J. O. Lindsay (ed.), *The New Cambridge Modern History: Vol. VII. The Old Regime 1713–1763*, Cambridge, 1966.

Biographical

38 Anderson, M. S., *Peter the Great*, 1978.
39 Cracraft, J., 'Some Dreams of Peter the Great: A Biographical Note' in *Canadian-American Slavic Studies*, vol. 8, no. 2 (Summer 1974).
40 Grey, Ian, *Peter the Great, Emperor of All Russia*, 1962.
41 Grunwald, C. de, *Peter the Great*, 1956.
42 Hatton R. H., *Charles XII of Sweden*, 1968.
43 Hughes, L., *Sophia, Regent of Russia*, New Haven, CT, 1990.
44 Lee, Stephen, *Peter the Great*, 1993.

45   Massie, R. K., *Peter the Great. His Life and World*, New York, 1980.
46   Pavlenko, N., *Petr Pervyi* [Peter the First], 1975 (excerpt in 20).
47   Schuyler, E., *Peter the Great, Emperor of Russia*, 2 vols, New York, 1884, rep 1967.
48   Sumner B. H., *Peter the Great and the Emergence of Russia*, 1951.
49   Troyat, H., *Peter the Great*, (English edn., New York, 1987).

Economic

50   Baykov, A., 'The Economic Development of Russia' in *Economic History Review* 2nd.series VII 137–49, reproduced in 51.
51   Blackwell, W. L. (ed.), *Russian Economic Development from Peter the Great to Stalin*, New York, 1974.
52   Blanc, S., 'The Economic Policy of Peter the Great', reproduced in 51.
53   Falkus, M. E., *The Industrialisation of Russia 1700–1914*, 1972.
54   Kahan, A., 'Continuity in Economic Activity and Policy during the post-Petrine period in Russia' in *Journal of Economic History* XXV (1965) 61–8, reproduced in 51.
55   Kahan, A., *The Plow, the Hammer and the Knout: An Economic History of Eighteenth Century Russia*, R. Hellie (ed.), Chicago, 1985.

Religious

56   Cracraft, J., 'Feofan Prokopovich' in 23.
57   Cracraft, J., *The Church Reform of Peter the Great*, Stanford, 1971.
58   Hosking, G. A., *Church, Nation and State in Russia and Ukraine*, 1991.
59   Muller, A. V., (tr.and ed.), *The Spiritual Regulation of Peter the Great*, Seattle, WA, 1972.
60   Sysin, F. E., 'The Formation of Modern Ukrainian Religious Culture: The Sixteenth and Seventeenth Centuries' in 58.

Military and naval

61   Anderson, R. C., *Naval Wars in the Baltic 1522–1850*, 1910.
62   Black, J., *A Military Revolution? 1550–1800*, 1991.
63   Bridge, C. A. G. (ed.), *History of the Russian Fleet during the Reign of Peter the Great by a Contemporary Englishman 1724*, 1899.
64   Frost, R., 'The Polish-Lithuanian Commonwealth and the "Military Revolution"' in J. S. Pula and M. B. Biskupski (eds), *Poland and Europe: Historical Dimensions*, New York, 1994.
65   Grey, I., 'Peter the Great and the Creation of the Russian Navy' in *History Today*, vol. 11, no. 9. (September 1961).
66   Hellie, R., 'Warfare, Changing Military Technology and the Revolution of Muscovite Society' in 68.

67 Keep, J. L., *Soldiers of the Tsar. Army and Society in Russia 1462–1874*, Oxford, 1985.
68 Lynn, J. A. (ed.), *Tools of War. Instruments, Ideas and Institutions of Warfare 1445–1871*, Champaign, IL, 1990.
69 Parker, G., *The Military Revolution 1500–1800*, Cambridge, 1988.
70 Parrott, D., 'The Military Revolution in Early Modern Europe' in *History Today*, vol. 42 (December 1992).
71 Woodward, D., *The Russians at Sea*, 1965.

Administration and opposition

72 Andrew, C. and Gordievsky, O., *KGB*, 1991.
73 Anisimov E. V., *The Reforms of Peter the Great; Progress Through Coercion in Russia*, St Petersburg 1989, (tr. J. T. Alexander, New York, 1993).
74 Bogoslovsky, M. M., *Petr Velikii I Ego Reforma* [Peter the Great and his Reforms], 1920 (excerpt in 20).
75 Chance, J. F. (ed.), *British Diplomatic Instructions 1689–1789 (Sweden Vol. I 1689–1727)*, 1922.
76 Cracraft, J., 'Opposition to Peter the Great' in E. Mendelsohn and M. S. Schatz, *Imperial Russia 1700–1917: State, Society and Opposition*, Champaign, IL, 1988.
77 Crumney, R. O., *Aristocrats and Servitors*, Princeton, 1983.
78 Hingley, R., *The Russian Secret Police, Muscovite, Imperial Russian and Soviet. Political Security Operations 1565–1970*, 1970.
79 Horn, D. B., *British Diplomatic Representatives 1689–1789*, 1932.
80 Meehan-Waters, B., 'Social and Career Characteristics of the Administrative Elite, 1689–1761' in 83.
81 Pavlov-Sil'vanzkii, N. P., 'Popular Reactions to Reform' in 34.
82 Peterson, C., *Peter the Great's Administrative and Judicial Reforms: Swedish Antecedents and the Process of Reception*, Stockholm, 1979.
83 Pintner, W. M. and Rowney, D. K., *Russian Officialdom: The Bureaucratisation of Russian Society from the Seventeenth to the Twentieth Century*, Chapel Hill, NC, 1980.
84 Pipes, R., *Russia under the Old Regime*, New York, 1974.
85 Yaney, G. L., *The Systematisation of Russian Government. Social Evolution in the Domestic Administration of Imperial Russia 1711–1905*, Champaign, IL, 1973.

Educational, cultural and scientific

86 Alexander, J. T., 'Medical Developments in Petrine Russia' in 20.
87 Boss, V., *Newton and Russia: The Early Influence 1694–1796*, Cambridge, MA, 1972.

88   Cracraft, J., *The Petrine Revolution in Russian Architecture*, Chicago, 1988.
89   Cross, A. G., *By the Banks of the Thames: Russians in Eighteenth Century Britain*, Newtownville, MA, 1980.
90   Marker, G., *Publishing, Printing and the Origins of Intellectual Life in Russia 1700–1800*, Princeton, NJ, 1985.
91   Okenfuss, M. J., 'Russian Students in Europe in the Age of Peter the Great' in 23.
92   Okenfuss, M. J., 'The Jesuit Origins of Petrine Education' in 23.
93   Phipps, J. F., (ed.), *Britons in seventeenth century Russia*, Ann Arbor, MI, 1922.
94   Raeff, M., 'The Enlightenment in Russia and Russian Thought in the Enlightenment' in 23.
95   Raeff, M., *Origins of the Russian Intelligentsia. The Eighteenth Century Nobility*, New York, 1966.
96   Talbot Rice, T., 'The Conflux of Influences in Eighteenth Century Russian Art and Architecture: A Journey from the Spiritual to the Realistic' in 23.

INDEX